WALTER REUTHER

GREAT MEN OF MICHIGAN
EDITED BY C. WARREN VANDER HILL

WALTER REUTHER

by

ROBERT L. TYLER

WILLIAM B. EERDMANS/PUBLISHER

PREFACE

This essay on the life of Walter P. Reuther claims no great originality. It is based entirely on the readily accessible public record that Reuther left behind in a veritable mountain of books, magazines, newspapers, publications of the labor press, government documents, and various autobiographical works of his contemporaries. It is also based on that more amorphous residue of memory from several decades of the author's reading in the reportage on Reuther's career. The author of this small addition to that voluminous bibliography intends then only an introduction, a placing, a tentative interpretation of an important career. The most the author can hope for is to arouse a curiosity for further reading and research.

Also, the author grew up in the era of the Great Depression and the Second World War and inhabited the same troubled world in which Reuther hewed out his historic place. To the author, Reuther was one of those historically significant persons, political forces, objects of public scorn or adulation, to which he half-consciously related in all those complex ways that contemporaries, unknown to each other, relate. In part, therefore, this brief essay is an attempt by the author to understand better a part of his era and one of the makers of its history. The passing of such a person as Walter Reuther makes for such punctuations not only in the flow of history but in the many, many biographies that compose it.

CHAPTER ONE

When Walter Reuther died in an airplane crash in May, 1970, Michigan lost one of its most famous and controversial adopted sons and the nation lost one of its most important and history-making labor leaders of the second third of the twentieth century. In one sense, with which we can all identify, no man's death ever comes at the right time. But in the healing impersonality of historical hindsight we can recognize that some deaths do come too soon, or too late, or at just the right time. John Keats, we might agree, died too soon. Adolph Hitler, alas, died too late. Abraham Lincoln perhaps died at the right time to insure his place in that "History" to which Secretary of War Stanton assigned him as he expired. Violent and arbitrary as an airplane crash is, we might still see Reuther's death, in the perspective of such "History," as having come at the right time. Or perhaps even a shade too late.

Reuther rose to prominence in American history on the wave of the labor revolution during the New Deal era. He was a peculiarly and appropriately tuned instrument for leadership in that revolution, and at that precise time. History and biography harmonized in his career. But by 1970, the year of his death, the times had changed. The labor movement no longer was the advance guard of social change and economic reform it had been in its years of struggle and glory. Reuther, even by the 1950's and 1960's, had perhaps begun to face that most frightening of possibilities, an intimation of irrelevance, a hunch that his time may have come and passed. Shortly before his death, in the spring of 1970, Reuther addressed an "environmental teach-in" on the University of Michigan campus in Ann Arbor. He warmed up and into his usually vigorous speech, urging his young audience to continue the good fight for human progress and freedom. All of Reuther's speeches, it has been said, became the same speech whatever the ostensible topic. The students listened good-naturedly to the rolling liberal-radical rhetoric and began to yell, "Right on, Walter!" Reuther apparently did not realize that he was being teased.

As we have suggested, history and biography seemed to come into perfect tune in the career of Walter Reuther. The history, like essential stage setting, we shall sketch in as we progress with this biographical essay. But whence came Walter Reuther, whose personality, style, commitment, and ideology fitted him so nicely to that history?

Walter was born September 1, 1907, the eve of Labor Day, into a family of high-thinking and plain-living working people in Wheeling, West Virginia. He was the second son in a family of four sons and a considerably younger daughter. His father, Valentine Reuther, had come to the United States as an eleven-year-old boy with his father, Jacob Reuther, in 1892. Valentine had grown up on a farm near the Wabash River in Illinois. Old Jacob Reuther, a white-haired, bearded patriarch, had left his poor dairy farm near Mannheim, Germany, to escape poverty and the Prussian conscription. Although only minimally schooled, Jacob was something of a self-made intellectual who had arrived at dogged Teutonic philosophical and religious positions as a pacifist and Christian Socialist. In Effingham, Illinois, he soon came to differ with the conservative Lutheran pastor. He took to writing out his long position papers to argue his basic case that the church should emphasize temporal injustices more than spiritual other-worldliness. He was probably unaware that the non-immigrant Protestant clergy of his day were making the same plea and calling their message the "Social Gospel." Finally, in protest, Jacob Reuther began to boycott the local Lutheran church and to conduct his own services in his home.

Young Valentine Reuther left home before 1900 to seek his fortune and, reversing the nineteenth century American migratory pattern, went east to find work in a steel mill in Wheeling, West Virginia. Perhaps we can find a symbol of America's big change from agrarian to industrial nation in young Valentine Reuther's eastward trek. Valentine went to work for less than $1.50 a day in wages. He soon did somewhat better as a beer wagon driver for the Schmulbach brewery of Wheeling, and he even found time after his long hours of work to involve himself in the local labor movement. He organized his fellow workers at the brewery into a local union. In 1904, only 23 years old, he was elected president of the Ohio Valley Trades and Labor Assembly. He became the persuasive spokesman to the press and before legislative committees for over forty local unions in the Wheeling area. He campaigned for Eugene V. Debs, the Socialist Party Presidential candidate, in 1904 and 1908. In the latter campaign he proudly rode the Party's famous "Red Special" railroad car as it passed through West Virginia. By that time, however, he had also married a young, red-haired German immigrant girl named Anna

8

Stocker, the daughter of a Swabian wagon maker. She had come to America to join a brother already here when her romance with a local swain in Germany had been vetoed by her father. Years later, when teased about being his wife's second choice, Valentine would remark gallantly that he would have been happy, if necessary, to have been Anna's third choice.

Valentine and Anna Reuther moved into a second floor apartment in a working class neighborhood. Anna settled quickly into her traditional role as commander of the *kinder, kirche,* and *kuche* fronts of the growing family. She brought to her job the same dutifulness and efficiency that Valentine brought to his beer wagon job, his lunchroom, his labor organizing, and his self-improvement. Like his father, and like his sons after him, Valentine was a determined self-improver. Though his formal education had been cut short when he moved to Wheeling from Effingham, Illinois, he continued to read and study and to collect an impressive private library of German classics and assorted books on the "social problem," both in English and German.

Walter was born into that formidable family and grew up in its rich but disciplined culture with no apparent adolescent crisis or rebellion. Valentine and Anna ran a strict household but with lots of genuine love and care. Walter once brought home some Hearst magazine during a labor boycott of Hearst publications. He suffered a whipping and a stern lecture on the ethics of labor solidarity, a somewhat excessive punishment for an inadvertent sin it might seem in our more latitudinarian era. However stern, and even pedantic, the atmosphere of the home may have been by latter-day standards of Dr. Spock, all the values thus inculcated were—perhaps ironically— those of democracy and equalitarianism, humanitarian concern for the underdog, the liberating mission of the labor movement, and all such ideas held together by the cement of self-discipline, self-improvement, duty and more duty.

The self-improvement in the Reuther household was thoroughly organized in the form of Sunday afternoon "seminars." After returning from church services—to which Valentine did not go in protest over an anti-union Labor Day sermon once delivered by the pastor— the family ate a substantial Sunday dinner, and the father and sons retired to an upstairs bedroom to hear the sons' assigned reports upon which they had worked all the previous week. The topics were always substantial and important: woman's suffrage, war and militarism, economic monopoly, the historic role of the labor movement. Walter and his brothers did their research after work in the local

9

Carnegie Public Library. Although Valentine had earlier led an unsuccessful fight to block the acceptance of Carnegie's tainted money for the Wheeling Public Library, he apparently acquiesced to it as a *fait accompli* and permitted his sons to use its resources. The Reuther sons invested great effort into their argumentative Sunday afternoon reports, and their father acted as a severe judge and critic of the substance, rhetoric, and delivery. Sometimes he would ask Walter or another of the sons to change sides, to argue the "affirmative" after having carefully prepared the "negative" all week.

Walter graduated from Ritchie Grammar School and entered Wheeling High School. He was not destined to finish. Economic pressures forced him to drop out and to take a job as an apprentice tool and die maker in the Wheeling Steel Corporation mill, the same mill his father had started his career in and where his older brother, Theodore, had already found a job. Because of the incredible working hours still prevailing at that time in the steel industry—seven-day weeks of twelve-hour days in some mills—Walter had to give up the weekly seminars. It was on this first job that Walter suffered an accident, a narrow escape indeed, which reveals an important aspect of his character, a trait which was to serve him well in an even more serious bodily injury—an assassination attempt—years later. A heavy die crashed to the floor and sheared off the big toe on one foot. Had the die fallen an inch closer it would have crushed the whole foot. Walter refused sedation and insisted that the severed and crushed toe be retrieved and brought to the hospital with him to be sewed back on. The operation, of course, was not a success. Years earlier Valentine Reuther had evidenced the same kind of stubbornness after a strange accident in his lunchroom. An exploding soda bottle had lodged slivers of glass in one eye. Valentine also had refused sedation and had ordered the slivers plucked out while he was held down on a table by force. His courage, however, had not saved the eye any more than Walter was to save his big toe by insisting upon an operation unheard of at that time.

There is an apocryphal story that Walter was discharged from his first job for trying to organize the workers into a boycott of Sunday and holiday work. The supposed boycott was for Columbus Day. But Walter denied the story. He quit the job on his own initiative to move to Detroit in early 1927 to try his luck in the bustling automobile industry. Such a move took a certain amount of blustering self-confidence because he had not completed the full course of his apprenticeship as a tool and die maker.

By the time Walter Reuther arrived in Detroit the city had been for more than a decade the automobile capital of the world. When Henry Ford began to make his famous Model T "Tin Lizzie" in 1908 he wrought a revolution in American society, and subsequently, the world, by making the new-fangled "horseless carriage" available to almost every American who could afford small monthly payments. Before this time, of course, the automobile had been largely a rich man's toy. Its ostentatious expense, as well as its noise and disturbing effect upon horses, had even led Woodrow Wilson to pontificate that it was the most important single thing turning resentful common people to Socialism. Ford accomplished his revolution through a ruthless rationalization of production, perfecting the already known but undeveloped system of putting together pre-manufactured, interchangeable parts on a continually moving assembly line. In 1914 he further rationalized the process by introducing almost simultaneously the spectacular $5.00 day and the speed-up. Thousands of workers were attracted to the Ford Company—and to Detroit, of course—by the unheard-of wages, and the relatively few workers actually hired were driven to the state of the "Ford jitters" by harsh and efficient plant foremen. Henry Ford's personal eccentricities—his stubborn conservatism in making style changes, his unwarranted interference in the personal lives of his employees, his crackpot and reactionary social and economic philosophy—more and more came to interfere with the efficient production of automobiles, as all his biographers concede. But in the first decade of the Model T, Ford was the undeniable revolutionary in the industry. By the 1920's, however, competitors began to press hard and to catch up. The basic idea of a cheap, mass-produced automobile could not long stay a Ford monopoly, and other companies quickly began to do the job much better than Ford. Reluctantly, in 1927, Ford decided to stop production of the Model T, virtually unchanged since the first of them rolled off the line in 1908, and to bring out a new model to try to regain an already lost competitive advantage.

When Walter Reuther arrived in Detroit in February, 1927, a very young-looking nineteen-year-old boy with flaming red hair and ruddy face, he found the city suffering an unemployment crisis brought on by the Ford Motor Company's closing. Ford had shut down completely to make the long and difficult changes which the shift from the Model T to the Model A required. Only small cadres of skilled workers found jobs, and thousands of Ford assembly line workers tramped the streets looking for work, forming long queues in the cold winter mornings in front of the employment offices in the city.

With more persistence than most, Walter appeared one morning at

11

4:30 at the employment office of the Briggs Manufacturing Company, an automobile body shop, and was hired for 85c an hour for the long thirteen-hour night shift. Even for the spartan Walter the job was gruelling. He went one long twenty-one-day stretch without a day off.

After two months at Briggs, Walter read an advertisement in the newspaper for skilled tool and die men to work on the Ford reconversion at the huge Highland Park plant. Walter showed up at the gate and was immediately told to "get the hell out of here" by the gigantic Ford Motor Company gatekeeper. Skilled tool and die men usually came middle-aged, with bald or greying pates, and slight, red-cheeked Walter was dismissed on sight as a bothersome and frivolous candidate for the advertised job. But he stayed. He argued two hours with the disdainful guard before he was finally admitted to the employment office. Inside the office the personnel officer reacted to Walter just as had the guard. But as a mechanic passed through the office carrying blueprints, Walter stopped him and persuaded the hiring officer and the mechanic to give him an impromptu test. He passed. He was grudgingly hired, on a two-day trial basis, as a bench hand at $1.05 an hour. Since the average hourly wage in the industry was about 50c, Walter suddenly found himself among the aristocracy of labor.

When he returned to the Briggs shop to clean out his locker, he discovered how valuable he had become to that employer. The foreman offered him a raise on the spot, and Sundays off. When Walter refused the offer, the foreman tried to stall by forbidding Walter from taking his lunch pail and possessions out of the plant. Again, for the third time that day, Walter had to argue long and persuasively to get his way. He finally had to spend some of his slender reserves on a taxicab to get back to the Highland Park Ford plant in time to begin his new job. Needless to say, Walter passed his two-day try-out test and was put on the permanent crew. He was to stay with the Ford Motor Company as a tool and die maker for the next five years, through the early years of the Great Depression.

During his first five-year stay in Detroit young Walter continued his dutiful self-improvement. Removal from the discipline of his family did not loosen any visible bonds, and Walter apparently kicked no traces. He did not live it up in the big city. The closest thing to dissipation he experienced apparently was what he and his brothers jokingly called their "whore-ology" tours late at night after work. They sought out these ladies of the night, not to purchase their wares but to engage them in conversation as amateur sociologists. For two years after he arrived in Detroit Walter even sent half his pay back to his father in Wheeling. When he reached his twenty-first birthday his father returned Walter's remittance and told him he had outgrown that familial obligation.

His long hours at Briggs and then at the Ford Highland Park plant left him little time for himself. He did join the YMCA and went there regularly to work out. On the brief questionnaire given him by the YMCA when he applied for membership he was asked what were his ambitions. He responded that he wanted to be either a labor organizer or a chicken farmer. Many years later automobile industry negotiators told him, a little wistfully perhaps, that he would have made an excellent chicken farmer.

He also resumed his formal education by enrolling in Fordson High School as a somewhat over-age student. He was able to attend classes because his shift at the Ford plant did not begin until late afternoon. In Fordson High School he met another older student, a former coal miner named Merlin Bishop, who became a close friend and who moved in to share an apartment with Walter and his two younger brothers, Roy and Victor. At the age of twenty-two Walter finally earned his high school diploma. He then enrolled in classes at Detroit's municipal university—now Wayne State University—and for a time identified himself in the school records as a "pre-law" student. At the University he helped organize a Social Problems Club, which then affiliated with the League for Industrial Democracy. The League was the campus "front" of the Socialist Party, sprung from the older Intercollegiate Socialist League, and which much later, in the 1960's, was to spawn the Students for a Democratic Society. Walter became the principal activist in the Social Problems Club. He helped to organize, for example, a protest over the exclusion of Negro students from a local hotel swimming pool that the University leased, and he led the fight to remove ROTC from the University. Walter, Merlin Bishop, and the younger brothers also plunged into the 1932 Presidential campaign for Norman Thomas, the candidate of the Socialist Party. They organized debates, speeches, and literature distributions. But despite their considerable efforts in the Detroit area—and the help of the Depression—Thomas won fewer than 40,000 votes in Michigan.

Reuther left the Socialist Party some years later as he became a famous and influential labor leader on the national scene, obviously considering the liberal wing of the Democratic Party a more realistic instrument for his political reformist ambitions than the increasingly moribund Socialist Party. But his youthful "radical" commitments

13

were regularly rediscovered by his many conservative enemies in later life and trotted out as propaganda weapons against him. Senator Barry Goldwater, for one, was an unrelenting political foe of Reuther in the 1950's—during the Senate hearings that preceded the passage of the Landrum-Griffin Act to control corruption in labor unions, for example—and used Reuther's undisguised "radical" past as ammunition in his attacks. Also, in the rabid, internecine factional warfare within the Left—especially during this period of the Depression—Reuther tended to be placatory and "ecumenical." Consequently there was not much documentary evidence to cite later of early, if only Left, "anti-Communism." It might be useful to sketch in the larger historical setting for Reuther's campaign work for Norman Thomas in 1932, and for his other youthful activities as a Socialist Party adherent. What did it mean for Walter Reuther to be a Socialist in 1932?

Before the First World War the international Socialist movement had a decidedly German cast to it. The German Social Democratic Party was the largest Socialist party in the world. Karl Marx and Friedrich Engels themselves—and the important succeeding intellectuals and theorists of Socialism, Karl Leibnicht, August Bebel, Karl Kautsky, Eduard Bernstein, *et al.*—had been Germans. Even in the United States the Socialist movement in its Marxist variant had been started by German immigrants, and the little Socialist Labor Party launched in the 1870's had been almost exclusively an immigrant and foreign language organization out of the mainstream of American politics. In the early 1900's, during the floruit of the American Socialist Party and the Presidential campaigns of Eugene Debs, for whom Valentine Reuther had worked so loyally in West Virginia, the Socialist movement "Americanized" itself considerably. But even then its greatest local successes came in such German enclaves as Milwaukee, Wisconsin. It was not therefore surprising that during the great xenophobic and patriotic binge of the First World War Americans became convinced that the presumed radical threat to their society was emanating from "pro-Germans" and apologists for the "Hun." Samuel Gompers, the shrewd and practical leader of the American Federation of Labor, even claimed to believe during those hysterical months that the whole international Socialist movement had been invented decades earlier by Chancellor Bismarck of the German Empire as a device for softening up the world for German conquest.

This peculiarly Teutonic Social Democracy—of which the three generations of Reuthers we have examined briefly are a fair sample—had by the early twentieth century created a whole working class culture, complete with songs, newspapers, a sacred history and hagiography, right doctrines and catechisms, a whole "way of life." In Germany itself the culture was anchored securely in the labor unions, which served as the mass electoral base for the political party. In the United States, of course, the movement and its culture never achieved that much everyday success and generality, except in its little immigrant enclaves such as Milwaukee or in its even smaller family cultures such as the Reuthers of Wheeling, West Virginia. The Socialist culture was, at least in its official doctrines, Marxist and revolutionary. The whole purpose of the movement obviously was to organize the working class, the "proletariat," for the accomplishment of its historic task, the revolutionary overthrow of "bourgeois" society and the ushering in of the next historic stage of human freedom. However officially revolutionary the movement claimed to be, it did not really live up to its revolutionary creed. To make an over-simple but perhaps illuminating analogy, the "Revolution" for good German Social Democrats was somewhat like the "Second Coming of Christ" for good evangelical Christians, something creedal and officially believed in but scarcely permeating everyday life and behavior. Everyday life for Socialists was May Day parades, picnics with beer, wurst, and potato salad, dutiful attendance at union meetings and social affairs, teaching one's children the true faith, singing the old labor hymns, and simply being a part of the movement.

The First World War shattered this almost-comfortable Socialist movement. Before the War the Second International—the loose organization of the Socialist parties of the world—met in periodic conventions and passed ringing resolutions calling for the overthrow of capitalism and for more particular ends. A frequent concern of the international movement was the threat of war and militarism, and some of the resolutions were addressed to that problem, as at Stuttgart in 1907. According to Marxist doctrine modern wars were brought on by the rivalries of capitalists for markets and raw materials and investment opportunities. The "proletariat had no fatherland" and had no business, obviously, supporting capitalist wars. If war came it would be the duty of all Socialists, and the working class in general, to withhold support of their countries' war efforts and to agitate for the working class revolution to end it. Such was the official doctrine. But 1914 was a debacle. Most Socialists jettisoned their internationalist doctrine and found reasons for rallying to their respective fatherlands' war efforts. The Socialist move-

15

ment never really recovered from this collapse. For the next generation, until the Second World War, the vanguard of international Socialism was no longer the solid German Social Democratic Party but rather the Bolsheviks, or Communists, of Russia who had actually made a revolution out of the troubles of the war. The new Communist movement in 1918 and 1919 recruited disgruntled revolutionary Socialists into its ranks, and these new Communist Parties in turn came together to form a new and purified Third International, or Comintern, from which the older Socialists who had betrayed the revolutionary moment were specifically barred.

Increasingly the various Communist Parties around the world became sycophantic dependents of the powerful and prestigious Communist Party of the U.S.S.R. As Stalin came to power over the revolution in Russia, he came also to use the international Communist movement as an instrument of Russian foreign policy, ordering it to pursue one "line," or program, during the 1928-1936 period, an entirely different policy in the 1936-1939 period, an even more cynically changed "line" in the 1939-1941 period, and a completely reversed "line" in the 1941-1946 period.

It was in the period of Walter Reuther's youth and young manhood that the rivalry and mutual distrust between Socialists and Communists was at its height. While Walter labored at the Highland Park plant of the Ford Motor Company and exercised at the YMCA, the Communist movement all over the world was berating Socialists as "Social Fascists," as untrustworthy betrayers of the workers who would fumble the revolutionary opportunity of the world Depression just as they had done during the First World War. Socialists, for their part, retaliated against Communists by calling them wreckers, anti-democrats, tyrants, and betrayers of the great humanist tradition of Socialism.

It was therefore in such a setting that Walter Reuther organized his Social Problems Club at Wayne University, campaigned for Norman Thomas and the Socialist Party in 1932, and carried on loyally the family traditions he had absorbed. Being interested primarily in the most practical side of politics and social reform, he probably bothered himself very little with all the bitter and angry polemics within the Left. There is little evidence that he either felt called upon to defend his Socialist tradition against the brickbats of the Communists or, conversely, considered for a moment that the Socialist tradition had indeed been discredited and dishonored as the Communists charged.

There are probably many different and subtle explanations pos-

16

sible to the psychoanalytical biographer for the calmness and apparent immunity from ideological storms that seem to have characterized Walter's Socialism in these years. For one thing, he was of that particular generation of Socialists too young to have experienced the disintegrating debacle of the war very intimately, but also too old to have been born into a post-war—and perhaps post-Socialist—family and climate of opinion. But the most persuasive explanation for Walter's apparently untroubled commitments, in that decade when commitments in general seemed most troubled, is found in his remarkable family and in his rearing. The winds of doctrine, and the storms of left-wing ideological controversy, apparently never touched him. He occupied a kind of eye of the storm, furnished like that upstairs bedroom of his boyhood where he and his brothers cozily argued their weighty subjects under the stern but doting supervision of Valentine Reuther.[1]

When Walter became president of the United Automobile Workers after the Second World War, long after he had become a prominent figure on the national labor scene, he proudly introduced his father and mother to the convention. However sentimental, and even cliché-ridden, the interlude in the proceedings of the convention may seem in cold print, the record does impart some of the sense of Walter's family culture and how it molded him for the rest of his life.[2]

PRESIDENT REUTHER: Now, I want to do something that will take a couple of minutes. It is a personal matter with me and I ask your indulgence. Down in the hills of West Virginia there is a little working-class family with a redheaded mother who raised a bunch of boys. She knows the problems of every working-class mother. She knows what it is to scrape and make ends meet. I remember one time when she bought a brand-new umbrella. We didn't have much money in our house in those days, and one of my kid brothers went out and tried to use it as a parachute and tore it apart. This working-class mother made a black shirt out of the cloth from that umbrella, because that's the way we lived in those days.

She has been a great inspiration to me, and at this time I want to present my mother to the Convention.

Mrs. Reuther was presented and acknowledged the introduction.

PRESIDENT REUTHER: The other member of my family I would like to present is one who is not unfamiliar with the struggles of the American workers. He is an old soapboxer, an old rabble-rouser who indoctrinated his boys when they were

17

pretty young, and he told them the thing most important in the world to fight for was the other guy, the brotherhood of man, and the Golden Rule. In 1923 he was the President of the Central Labor Body in my home town of Wheeling, West Virginia. I advise you not to yell for a speech when I introduce this fellow, because he may make one.

At this time I want to present a good pal of mine, an old fighter in the ranks of labor, a Trade-unionist from away back when the going was rough. I give you at this time my father, Val Reuther.

I warned you fellows—I am not responsible for anything he may say.

MR. VAL REUTHER: Ladies and Gentlemen, Delegates to the UAW-CIO Convention: Permit me to assure you that it has been a pleasure for Mrs. Reuther and me to spend the closing days of this Convention with you. It reminds me of my younger years. I can assure you I am extremely happy that the seed that I have tried to sow in the minds of our children as they grew up from childhood is bearing fruit. I am happy beyond the power of words to see that they are engaged in the trade-union movement that has always been dear and close to my heart, and I am extremely happy that this organization with which they are affiliated is part of the CIO, because they express the sentiment and the trade-union spirit that I believe in—the industrial form of organization. I am proud that your great organization has taken a definite and uncompromising stand against the question of discrimination against minorities. Those who take the opposite stand are on the wrong side. Their attitude is indefensible and inexcusable.

You can only build a strong labor movement by uniting every man and woman who works for wages, whether it is in the factory, in the mines, on the farm, or in the office. . . .

In conclusion may I urge you delegates, representing as I understand 900,000 members, to be constant in your loyalty and devotion to the trade-union movement, for it is not only the vehicle and the highway that leads to a better life, it is the beacon light pointing the way to a richer, a fuller, and a more abundant life. Be loyal to it.

Thank you.

PRESIDENT REUTHER: I am glad he is not a delegate to the Convention. I want to say in all sincerity that in his day he was one of the best in the front lines of labor's struggles.

I will recognize this Brother at the rear mike.

DELEGATE FLEMING, LOCAL 34: I would like to move that we give the father of our leader, our great President, an honorary lifetime membership in our UAW-CIO.

The motion was supported.

18

PRESIDENT REUTHER: I will recognize that motion, provided it is distinctly and clearly understood that he cannot run against me for President.

All those in favor of the motion to bestow on my father a lifetime honorary membership—which I deeply appreciate—all those in favor signify by saying aye. . . . Those opposed. . . . *The motion was unanimously carried.*

PRESIDENT REUTHER: It is so ordered: and thank you from the bottom of my heart.

At this time I want to take just a moment to call upon. . . *A delegate called out for the father of President Reuther to make another speech.*

PRESIDENT REUTHER: I am afraid to get him back here again. I know him much better than you fellows do. My mother will say, "There he goes again, when you get the old fellow wound up he never knows when to stop."

CHAPTER TWO

In the ceaseless transitoriness that is history every moment can in theory be isolated as a "turning point" if so desired. But in long hindsight some moments seem more pregnant with great change than others, and for both Walter Reuther and the world he inhabited the early months of 1933 were such a time. On January 30th the aging President of the Weimar Republic of Germany, Paul Von Hindenberg, appointed Adolph Hitler as Chancellor, and almost immediately Hitler began to concoct the crises which were to make him dictator with the power to work out his evil ambitions. On March 4th, President-elect Franklin D. Roosevelt took the oath of office at the depth of the Depression and tried in his inaugural speech to inspire a dejected and anxious American people on the brink of economic collapse. In the Soviet Union, Joseph Stalin had already consolidated his power over rival claimants to the mantle of Lenin. He had completed the first of the Soviet Union's draconian "Five Year Plans" and had already launched the second. He was already brooding, in all probability, over the hypothetical plots against him and preparing the reign of terror and the purges of the mid-1930's. In January, 1933, Walter Reuther was fired from his job at the Ford Motor Company. He was twenty-five years old.

19

Walter did not know exactly why he was fired. It may have transpired that the company learned of his labor union sympathies and activities, or of his scarcely secret attachment to the Socialist Party. Or his discharge could have been merely another unremarkable cutting-back caused by the deepening Depression, by the sharp curtailment of production and sales in the automobile industry. In any event, Walter never learned the real reason for his peremptory severance.

But he was not really too unhappy with the change in his circumstances. It offered him the sudden freedom to do something he and his brother Victor had for some time talked of doing, but which they would have been reluctant to do while still enjoying the luxury during the Depression of having jobs. They decided to take a tour of the world, a twentieth century and working class equivalent of the gentleman's Grand Tour of the eighteenth century. A member of the Communist Party and a fellow automobile worker in Detroit, John Rushton, had taken a job in the Soviet Union at the new Molotov Automobile Works in Gorki. He had discovered the job through his Party connections, of course, and through Amtorg, the trading corporation of the Soviet Union in the United States. He had then recruited Walter and Victor Reuther. As a skilled tool and die maker, Walter was precisely the kind of worker the Soviet planners were seeking. Because Walter had such leverage with his skill he was able to persuade the Amtorg recruiters to take his brother, Victor, as well, although Victor was only an assembly line worker that the Russians otherwise might not have been interested in.

This stint of work in the Soviet Union by the Reuther brothers came to play a recurring and controversial part in the subsequent careers of the two. The whole affair, as well as a controversial letter supposedly written by Walter to his friend Merlin Bishop in Detroit, was to come up over and over again in their later careers. Mostly the Russian adventure—and the letter in several versions—was to serve as conservative ammunition against Walter, to prove that he was a Communist, or at least a Communist sympathizer. We have already placed young Walter, as a Socialist, in the sectarian jungle of the Left in the early 1930's, and we need not recapitulate that story. But even if Reuther's reputed sympathy for Communism, charged by his later right-wing critics, was correct, he certainly outgrew the infatuation. At the height of his career he was certainly never accepted as a "Communist" by the critics on his left. Indeed, at the height of his fame in the late 1940's and early 1950's—when the Cold War and anti-Communism were running at full tide—Walter became one of the national leaders of the vigorous and sophisticated "Anti-Communist Left." But at this juncture it is enough to tell the story of the Reuther boys' junket and to deal with the controversies it engendered as they arise later in the story and in the factional history of the United Automobile Workers.

Ironically, the Ford Motor Company, which had just fired Walter and which obviously had no sympathy with the ideologies of either Reuther or the Soviet Union, had already made a business arrangement with the Soviet Union through Amtorg to help in the building and launching of the Molotov Automobile Works in Gorki to which Walter was going. Ford had agreed to sell its Model A dies and production equipment to the Soviet Union. But with perhaps excessive caginess the Ford Company delayed the delivery of the materials until its own new V8 model was in full production, as if it feared some market competition from the Soviet Union.

Walter and Victor withdrew the $1600 they had saved during their five years in Detroit and went home to Wheeling to break the news of their trip to their not entirely enthusiastic father. They informed their father of the full sweep of their planned itinerary only in bits and pieces, letting him adjust to one bit of data before giving him the next. While in Wheeling, Walter also took Victor around to the machine shop in the Wheeling High School to give him some hurry-up lessons in basic machinist's skills. Then, on February 16, 1933, they set sail from New York in a German ship. They disembarked eight days later in Hamburg to begin their great adventure.

They arrived in Germany, of course, within a month after the ascension to the Chancellorship by Adolph Hitler. In that first fateful month the Nazis—as many historians still claim—set fire to the Reichstag building in Berlin, claimed that the arson had been the work of Communists planning to trigger a revolution, then moved quickly to "save" Germany from that fearful threat in the nick of time. In Berlin, Walter and Victor took a tour of the Reichstag ruins under the guidance of Storm Troopers who gave the official propaganda spiel. The ashes were hardly cold.

After arriving in Germany the brothers learned that Amtorg was delaying their reception in Gorki for lack of facilities to house foreign workers. They found themselves therefore up against an indefinite wait to get to their destination. But they made quick plans to use the time to best advantage. They would explore Germany and visit as many other European countries as they could during the wait. They did decide, however, to cut short their tour of Berlin

21

rather precipitously. Upon arriving, they had taken lodgings in a hostel that catered to radical youth—hardly the most popular people in Germany as the Third Reich began. One night the hostel was raided by Storm Troopers, and Walter and Victor avoided being roughed up—or worse—by slipping through a rear window.

They left Berlin thereupon to visit the south of Germany and their mother's native village of Sharnhausen. There they were grateful to discover that their uncles and aunts and cousins were all staunchly anti-Nazi working people, all save one uncle who was the vice mayor of the village. In Sharnhausen they took two of their pretty cousins to the movies and again ran into the hostility of the Nazis. When the lights went up in the theatre the crowd rose to its feet and burst into the Horst Wessel Lied, the Nazi Party song commemorating the "martyrdom" of one of its early street fighters who had been killed in a rumble with Communists, or some such enemies of Germany. The Reuther brothers and the cousins remained seated, rather ostentatiously in the crowded theatre. The angry mutterings around them became so threatening that they began finally to jabber loudly in English to each other to indicate that they were tourists or outsiders. Also, they witnessed a Nazi rite in which some Storm Troopers put the torch to a great pile of trade union banners, perhaps to ceremonialize the abolition of the trade unions and the Social Democratic Party and their replacement by the National Socialist Labor Front. Two labor union members, moved by sentiment more than prudence, tried to rescue the banners from the flames. The Storm Troopers beat them severely.

From Stuttgart they embarked on a tour of eleven countries, mostly by bicycle. The tour took them into Austria, Italy, France, England, and the smaller countries in between and contiguous. In Italy they listened to a bombastic public address by Benito Mussolini. In England they cycled to the usual tourist sites within their reach and also paid calls on local labor leaders to discuss trade union problems.

In December, 1933, they finally received their Russian visas. They caught a train for Moscow in Berlin and made the long trip across Poland in the bitter cold. When they arrived in Moscow the temperature was thirty-five degrees below zero. Without waiting to see the tourist sites of Moscow they proceeded directly to Gorki, about two hundred miles further east. Gorki was the old pre-Revolutionary city of Nizi-Novgorod. While riding in a crowded trolley car in Gorki they had their pockets picked, an inauspicious beginning to their stay.

The residence for foreign workers was a large two-story building resembling an army barracks. They moved into a part of the building named "Commune Ruthenberg," after an early leader of the American Communist Party, but which was more informally called the "American Village." They soon learned that the little colony of foreign workers was divided into two types, the politically indifferent who had come merely for the adventure and to sell their skills where needed, and the politically sympathetic, either members of various European Communist parties or "fellow travellers."

The factory itself could only have disappointed them, after the sophisticated production system they were used to in Detroit. For one thing, the Molotov works in Gorki were unheated. Production workers had to do their tasks on the line and somehow keep warm as best they could, bundled up in sheepskin-lined arctic clothing. Walter could duck into the heat treatment room periodically to warm up because he was somewhat more mobile as a skilled worker. Also, the production schedules were delayed by the procrastination of the Ford Motor Company in sending the promised Model A dies. But production was hampered even more by all the difficulties attendant upon trying to organize and run a complex automobile assembly factory with inexperienced managers and workers.

Walter wanted to be understanding and enthusiastic—personality traits, of course, which he brought to any situation. He found himself appointed leader of a sixteen-man shock troop or workers' brigade. He became a Stakhanovite worker, the name deriving from that quota-busting, speed-up hero of the First Five Year Plan. Walter regularly earned a little red burlap flag on his bench, the reward, like a schoolboy's gold star, for his efficient work. Discovering that there was an English language newspaper, the *Daily News,* published in Moscow for all the English-speaking workers in Russia, he began to contribute articles to it. In one of his helpful essays he criticized some particularly inefficient practice in the management of the Molotov works in Gorki. He was somewhat chagrined to learn that the foreman of the foreign workers in Gorki received a stern reprimand from his superiors in the Plan on the strength of the article.

The two brothers learned of the sternness of the Communist Party on several other occasions. The Party was still halfway in its evolution from Lenin's revolutionary vanguard to that toadying bureaucracy it became during and after the Stalin Terror. They sat through an ideological self-criticism and "cleansing" session of the Molotov workers and saw fifteen percent of the Communist Party members expelled for a wide variety of political and technological sins. They also saw—or perhaps more accurately, heard—the secret police arrest an Italian worker in the foreign workers' barracks at three o'clock in the morning. Nobody heard any more of the man, nor did anybody talk about him thereafter.

They also, admittedly, enjoyed the company of Russian girls in Gorki, although they claimed that no serious attachments developed. Years later, however, after Nikita Khrushchev's celebrated visit to the United States in 1959 and his almost equally celebrated debate with Walter Reuther at a dinner party, the trade union newspaper of the Soviet Union, *Trud,* published charges against Reuther by a woman signing herself "N." She and Walter had been married in Gorki, she claimed. Walter had wooed her persistently, and he had promised undying fidelity. The fact that she never heard from him again after he left Gorki was only to be expected, she argued, from such unreliable persons as Social Democrats. If they would sell out the working class they could be expected to sell out on their personal commitments. Of course "N's" charges got back to the United States, and Walter denied them categorically. Even the Detroit *News,* not always a Reuther defender, agreed with him that he was probably not a bigamist.

As their contract period for work came to an end the two brothers decided to use their otherwise unspendable ruples on an extended tour of the Soviet Union, and then to return to the United States by way of Asia and the Pacific. They left Gorki and Moscow for a leisurely swing through southern Russia, and then they returned to Moscow to pick up the Trans-Siberian Railroad for Manchuria, already gobbled up by the Japanese Empire and renamed Manchukuo. From Manchuria they made their way into China proper, to Nanking from where they took a river boat to Shanghai on the coast. They witnessed, with horror, the bearded, turbanned Sikh deck hands on the river boat clubbing the starving Chinese back into the water as they swam out to the boat. From Shanghai they sailed for Japan. They made a quick bicycle tour of parts of that country. In Yokohama they found jobs as deck hands on the steamer *President Harding.* They arrived in San Francisco late in 1935, after almost three years of adventure and education in almost all the countries of Europe, in the Soviet Union, and in China and Japan. The experience was to be of incalculable value to Walter and his brother, supplying a storehouse of memories and cases in point to enrich and deepen already established commitments to the urgency of material human betterment.

During his stay in Gorki, Walter wrote an enthusiastic, almost

24

boyish, letter to his friend Merlin Bishop back in Detroit. Whatever the original, or actual, letter said—and Walter later disavowed all the differing versions published by his political enemies in and out of the United Automobile Workers union—it became one of the dogged "scandals" in his later life. The letter ends with a salute: "Carry on the fight for a Soviet America. Vic and Wal." The letter, or different versions of it, appeared first as anti-UAW propaganda during the 1937 sit-down strikes in the automobile industry. It then appeared in the records of the National Labor Relations Board hearings over the labor problems of the Ford Motor Company, in the 1941 political campaign literature of the anti-Reuther forces in the UAW, in the organs of the Detroit press, in a *Saturday Evening Post* article, in the reports of the Committee on Un-American Activities of the House of Representatives under Martin Dies, and in other places. In the National Labor Relations Board hearings Walter was asked directly by the Ford counsel whether he had written the version he was shown, and Walter denied having done so. Whatever enthusiastic and uncritical letters Walter may have written home from Russia— and in a footnote to the *Saturday Evening Post* article Walter admitted that such letters may indeed have been written—the various circulating versions of the "Vic and Wal" letter were very likely distortions, perhaps including that final phrase which urged a "Soviet America."[1]

From hindsight now the whole storm seems vapid and ridiculous. In the political context of the 1940's and 1950's it was damning indeed to have it on one's record that he had once favored a "Soviet America." But in the context of the 1930's, and from the hand of a young man like Walter Reuther, an ecumenical Socialist visiting the land of the only existing Socialist revolution, the remark, even if genuine, seems neither very heinous nor shocking.

When Walter returned to Detroit in early 1936 he found it almost impossible to find work. In three years the New Deal had alleviated some of the pains of mass unemployment but had not solved the problem. But Walter had other urgent things to do during his unemployment. He hitchhiked to various towns giving lectures for a Quaker group, attended the convention in Columbus, Ohio, which began the American Student Union, and taught a brief summer course at Commonwealth College in Mena, Arkansas. It was a time to adjust to his re-entry into American society and a time to digest the experiences of the previous three years, which he did typically by stepping up his activities, by moving around and talking.

While riding on a trolley car in Detroit early in 1936 he saw and

25

recognized a girl he had known three years earlier before his trip to Europe. May Wolf was a teacher of physical education in the public schools and an organizer for the American Federation of Teachers. She had also been active in the little Proletarian Party of Michigan. Obviously Walter and May found much to talk about. They began to see each other often and regularly. On March 13, 1936, after a brief courtship, they were married. From the beginning of their married life they led a spartan existence, hurrying from place to place to attend meetings or to give speeches, sometimes getting only a few hours sleep before a new day of hurried activities began.

Before and after his interlude of teaching in Arkansas in the summer of 1936, Walter began to devote much time to the new automobile workers union, which was in the middle of its early and complicated growing pains. Although unemployed and without the constituency of a local union, Walter met with the early leaders in Detroit and joined with them in planning how the union might end its stultifying sponsorship by the American Federation of Labor. By 1936 Walter had found his cause and the organization to which he was to devote the rest of his life.

But what had been happening during his three years away from the United States? To the country in general? To the labor movement?

He had left the country in early 1933, at the very depth of the Depression, during that interregnum after the election of Franklin D. Roosevelt and before his Inauguration on March 4, 1933. Walter missed, of course, the frantic months after the inspiring Inaugural Address in which the New Deal had emerged, and he missed that false dawn of hope—but nevertheless a dawn—for the labor movement of the National Industrial Recovery Act, with its Section 7A, which for the first time, if only on paper, made it the law of the land that labor would have the right to organize and to bargain collectively without interference.

> Section 7A read: Employees shall have the right to organize and bargain collectively, through representatives of their own choosing, and shall be free from the interference, restraint or coercion of employers of labor, or their agents, in the designation of such representatives or in self-organization or in other concerted activities. . . .

The promise of Section 7A, however, was scarcely fulfilled, except perhaps in the coal mining fields where John L. Lewis started a massive organizational drive for his United Mine Workers under the slightly hyperbolic slogan, "The President wants you to join the

Union." But elsewhere American industry, organizing under their NRA codes or the government's eventual "blanket code," heeded only the letter of Section 7A and not its spirit. Various "employee representation" plans grew in profusion across the nation—"company unions," in the older disparaging terminology of the independent labor movement—to meet the minimal requirements of the law. The National Labor Board established by the NRA to administer these labor provisions of the law tended to uphold "company unions" as being in compliance with the law. President Roosevelt himself seemed disinterested in this question of real versus token representation and in a famous news conference said somewhat impatiently that the law, as far as he was concerned, permitted workers to choose the "Sultan of Swat," as the famous Yankee slugger Babe Ruth was known, to represent them if they so desired.

Besides the permissiveness of the government in interpreting the Section 7A labor provisions of the law, the structural and temperamental conservatism of the existing labor movement, represented mostly by the American Federation of Labor, stood in the way of any dramatic growth and expansion. As the name implies, the American Federation of Labor was a federation of existing national and "international" (with Canadian locals) trade unions. From the beginning the AFL was dominated by the skilled craft unions, mostly in the building trades. Such unions were unready by inclination and ideology to embark on a vigorous program to organize the unorganized workers, most of whom, of course, were unskilled or semi-skilled production workers in the great mass production industries such as steel, automobiles, chemicals, rubber, electrical supplies and communications. If such workers organized, even under the protecting wing of the new law, where would they go? Into which existing unions? Did any existing craft union really want them? Such were the frustrations that began to rend the labor movement even under the tentative and unenforced Section 7A of the NIRA from 1933 to 1935.

In 1935 the whole NIRA, including its Section 7A, was struck down by the Supreme Court. But even before the Court had delivered its coup de grâce to the experiment, the whole grandiose plan had begun to crumble of its own weight and unenforceability. Senator Robert Wagner of New York wished to save something of the experiment even before it collapsed or before the Supreme Court killed it. He wished to rescue the central idea of Section 7A. Early in 1935 he introduced a bill, the National Labor Relations Act, commonly called the Wagner Act, to prohibit certain "unfair labor practices" to the end that workers would be free from interference

27

or reprisal to organize or join unions of their own choosing. To enforce these protections the law would establish a regulatory commission called the National Labor Relations Board with all the powers of federal commissions to adjudicate and order, subject, of course, to the parties' right to appeal in the federal courts.

In hindsight Senator Wagner's bill was one of the most important laws of the whole New Deal era, with quick and deep effects upon American society. Oddly enough it was largely Senator Wagner's own idea. It had not been prepared as a part of President Roosevelt's legislative program, and the President was scarcely forewarned of it. Roosevelt was, in fact, not very enthusiastic about the bill as it progressed through the Congressional machinery toward passage, until at the last moment he joined the bandwagon and urged Congress to pass it. Congress reviewed the bill without the kind of divisive debate the legislation might seem to warrant, and it passed both houses with comfortable majorities. The unfulfilled promise of Section 7A was now to be fulfilled, although employers tended for the first couple of years to resist the law on the expectation that the Supreme Court would invalidate it as it had the NIRA. Opposition began to collapse in 1937 after the Supreme Court in the Jones and Laughlin Steel Co. case unexpectedly upheld the law. In the meantime the labor movement, under the leadership of John L. Lewis, and under the protection of the new law, wrought its "revolution" in American society. It was a revolution in which Walter Reuther was to emerge as a national leader.

John L. Lewis, as we have seen, had taken early advantage of the Section 7A opportunity, and under the Wagner Act he continued to urge his fellow labor leaders in the AFL to do likewise. Other leaders of "industrial" unions within the AFL joined Lewis. Their aim was to organize the millions of workers in the mass production industries into new industry-wide unions which would transcend the outdated and restrictive craft limitations of the old trade unions. If workers in the automobile industry, for example, had to be parcelled out to separate craft unions of machinists, painters, carpenters, upholsterers, electricians, janitors, and so on, then the workers of the automobile industry would never be organized and the beckoning opportunities of, first, Section 7A and then the Wagner Act would be squandered. Lewis and his lieutenants argued that only "industrial," or "vertical," unions would satisfy the historic reality and the opportunity. All workers who contributed to the making of an industrial product, from the secretaries in the front office to the janitors that swept up after the last shift, belonged logically in the same union.

At the 1934 convention of the AFL in San Francisco, Lewis and his followers won only a weak concession from the leadership, who agreed with obvious reluctance to the granting of charters for unions in the automobile, rubber, cement, radio, and aluminum industries, but with the impossible provision that all existing jurisdictional rights of existing craft unions must be respected.

The following year, after months of delay and inaction by the appointed leaders of thousands of newly organized workers, Lewis went to the AFL convention in Atlantic City with a demand for real action. The dilatory tactics, Lewis charged, resulted in the new industrial unions, with their thousands of eager but increasingly disaffected members, "dying like the grass withering before the autumn sun." The fight waxed very bitter in Atlantic City, and became even physical as Lewis and William L. Hutcheson of the Carpenters' Union engaged in brief verbal insults and their famous fisticuffs. Put off by the convention, their program for industrial unionism voted down, Lewis and his followers then met to decide what to do. In November, 1935, about a month before Walter and Victor Reuther returned to San Francisco on the *President Harding,* Lewis announced the formation of the Committee for Industrial Organization, still ostensibly within the AFL. After succeeding months of further conflict, jurisdictional disputes, resignations and suspensions, the executive council of the AFL, in March, 1937, formally expelled all the new CIO unions from any association with the AFL. In 1938 the Committee for Industrial Organization met in convention and renamed itself the Congress of Industrial Organizations.[2]

Thus by early 1936, when Walter reappeared in Detroit, the bitter conflict between the AFL establishment and the new CIO-organized industrial unions had already scarred the labor movement in the automobile industry. While Walter had been helping the Russians make their copy of the Ford Model A in Gorki, labor organizers had met an enthusiastic reception among automobile workers in the United States. The first optimism of Section 7A swept through the industry. Many spontaneous strikes by automobile workers in 1934 evidenced a real interest in organization and, already, a growing irritation with the AFL leadership. By 1935 the irritation had become disillusion. For example, a poll taken in 1935 by the short-lived National Automobile Labor Board of the NRA showed a

29

majority of the automobile workers preferring no union at all over the AFL. The "Federal" locals of the AFL were merely holding expedients under appointed leaders. Their sole purpose seemed to be to collect the dues of initially enthusiastic workers until the leaders could decide how to parcel them out among existing unions.

In May, 1936, automobile workers with sympathies toward the new CIO planned means of taking control of the union at the convention in South Bend, Indiana. Walter Reuther, although still without employment and consequently a member of no local, went to the convention as the delegate from a General Motors local in Detroit. His credentials were challenged, but he claimed that he had worked briefly for General Motors in late 1935 and early 1936 under an assumed name. He was seated without further challenge. Reuther claimed later that "the guys" had wanted him as their delegate and that it had not even been his own idea to go the convention. He had been chosen by one of the little cabals that had organized for the job of rescuing the foundering United Automobile Workers from the dead hand of the AFL. Walter never evinced much guilt about the subterfuge, or about his technical ineligibility. The secretary of the local gave him five dollars from her purse for expenses. He was enjoined to return unspent money.

CHAPTER THREE

The 1936 convention of the UAW in South Bend, Indiana, to which Walter Reuther went on his dubious credentials, faced big decisions. The convention proved the turning point in the history of unionization in the automobile industry. The UAW at this convention took over its own governance from the AFL, elected its own officers for the first time, and began its association with the Committee on Industrial Organization, which itself had only recently been founded by John L. Lewis. The delegates elected Homer Martin, a former Missouri Baptist minister and the incumbent AFL-appointed vice-president, as their new president. The new vice-president was Wyndham Mortimer, an experienced labor organizer allegedly in the orbit of the Communist Party. George Addes became secretary-treasurer. Walter Reuther was elected to the executive board.

Almost as if liberated by this convention, the UAW sprang into life again, and quickly grew in numbers to regain and surpass its 1933 to 1935 membership before the disillusionment with the AFL had begun to set in. Within a few months of the convention the UAW was to challenge the mighty General Motors and Chrysler corporations and to win astonishing partial victories in the resulting struggles.

Up to this moment in time the relatively new and expanding automobile industry had successfully resisted unionization. The industry recruited most of its labor force, black and white, from the rural South and from Appalachia. Employers—Henry Ford when he dominated the early pioneer years of the industry—saw to it that these docile immigrants, new to the big city and to the factory, came in much greater numbers than there were jobs available. Henry Ford's famous $5.00 a day policy for workers in 1914, for example, attracted thousands of eager job seekers at the same time the spectacular pay raise was accompanied by a cost-cutting speed-up, a further rationalization of the assembly line, and a reduction in the Ford labor force. Even in the Depression years, when nearly a quarter of a million persons were on relief in Detroit, automobile company recruiters went into the deep South and into Appalachia to draw Negroes and "hillbillies" into the labor force of Detroit. Southern Negroes scarcely needed to be recruited, however, because the Depression and the already beginning revolution in the commercial agriculture of the South were forcing white and Negro sharecroppers into a migration that has become one of the great demographic revolutions in the history of twentieth century America.

Any noticeable dissatisfaction with the job on the part of automobile workers led to quick dismissal and to the hiring of somebody else from this labor reservoir. With the continuing rationalization of the assembly line in the industry, the work in an automobile plant grew more nerve-racking and more achingly dull. Foremen and supervisors enforced a rigid discipline. At the Ford Motor Company the discipline even followed the worker into the parking lot and to his home. The early Ford "Sociology Bureau" checked to see that workers owning cars owned only Fords, that they led exemplary, moral lives at home, eschewing tobacco and alcoholic beverages, and that they tended their household gardens that Henry Ford thought desirable. Workers in the automobile industry—as even the flashy $5.00 a day Ford wage of 1914 indicates—earned relatively high pay

31

compared to other industrial workers in America, but the hourly wage rate did not reflect the average *annual* wage of automobile workers, which in the 1930's was only about $1100, about at the poverty level. Workers, of course, were frequently laid off in the seasonal production schedules of the industry. The laying-off was usually arbitrary and capricious, based on who the worker "knew" or how well his personal relations with the foreman had been going. There was obviously no union-maintained seniority system. Job security was virtually nonexistent.[1]

Labor organization made slow progress in this insecure, seasonal, authoritarian industry, with its always available reservoir of docile job seekers. But workers did have real grievances, however impossible it was to express them. When the National Industrial Recovery Act became law, automobile workers showed considerable spontaneous interest in Section 7A with its seeming protection for their right to organize. In 1933, for example, the industry experienced a rash of wildcat strikes, and these uprisings closed down a hundred plants for brief periods during the year. The American Federation of Labor responded rather sleepily to this opportunity. William Collins, the man appointed by the national AFL leaders to coordinate the organizational drive in the automobile industry, would typically call a meeting at a plant, or would be invited to a plant by some committee of workers interested in forming a labor union. At the organizational meeting, hundreds of curious and interested workers would turn out to listen to Collins. Many would then sign up as members in the AFL, in hastily designated "Federal" locals to which the AFL would appoint officers. These appointed leaders would then proceed to negotiate with employers for "stabilization" agreements which increasingly seemed to the workers to be only assurances to employers that they had nothing to fear from the organization. For its part, the AFL seemed more interested in signing up members and collecting dues than in pressing for redress of grievances. Also, the AFL seemed embarrassed, to the point of bickering among themselves, over what to do with the hundreds of new automobile workers. How would they all be parcelled out to the existing craft unions of the AFL? Very quickly automobile workers became disillusioned with the AFL.

In June, 1934, 157 delegates from half as many local unions met in Detroit. Although all these local unions had some "Federal" affiliation with the AFL, the delegates revealed their true feelings about the affiliation when they voted to bar all AFL agents and observers from their deliberations. The convention sent an inquiry to John L. Lewis, who was already preparing his program for industrial unions for the next AFL convention. The AFL was almost completely discredited by the spring of 1935. Francis Dillon, appointed director of the automobile federal locals, ended a spontaneous strike of 30,000 workers by accepting a weak arbitration offer by the employees. Thereafter automobile locals began to revolt openly. The National Automobile Labor Board, a short-lived commission of the NRA, conducted a poll in early 1935 which showed that eighty-eight percent of the workers favored "no union" to only eight percent favoring the AFL. Labor historians do not interpret this poll as revealing any real anti-union sentiment, only an anti-AFL opinion.

Despite the reluctance of the national AFL leaders, they had to agree in August, 1935, to the granting of a charter for a new United Automobile Workers union. The AFL then appointed Francis Dillon to be its president and Homer Martin its vice-president and granted the new union a "probationary" status within the AFL. No jurisdictional rights of any existing craft unions in the AFL, moreover, could be sacrificed to the new automobile union.

Two months later, we have noted, John L. Lewis resigned from the executive council of the AFL and established his new Committee on Industrial Organization. At the plant level, automobile unions began to ignore their nominal AFL affiliation and to turn to Lewis and the new CIO. With the May, 1936, convention in South Bend approaching, the locals also began to organize their delegates to make sure of accomplishing their main purpose, to end AFL supervision and to elect their own officers. Thus, it was during this turning point in the labor story that Walter Reuther returned from his wanderings, revived his old connections in Detroit, and was selected "by the guys," as he put it, to be their delegate to the convention. His absence of credentials appeared, under the circumstances, to be a minor technicality.

But after the convention and his elevation to the executive board of the UAW, Reuther had no more problems with his status. He became, of course, a paid, professional official of the UAW. He had a job and a mission. When he returned to Detroit to organize and amalgamate the West Side locals, he rented an office at 35th Street and Michigan Avenue. It was barely more than a cubbyhole. From the locals under his tutelage he created West Side Local 174, which soon became a very big local in the UAW. He began the task with only seventy-eight members to work with, but very soon, by the end of 1936, he had 30,000 members in the local. He did all his own office work. He typed and penned drafts of leaflets and speeches, issued press releases, corresponded and talked with his fellow UAW officials and with the rank and file. For Reuther, and others in the UAW, it was the early heroic age, the "good old days" when the union was David to the corporations' Goliath. In Reuther's mind and memory it also thereafter tended to be the ideal way of unionization. As a later leader of "Big Labor" he more than once made public his misgivings about the changes that had occurred, and he felt particularly guilty about big AFL-CIO conferences on expense accounts in such places as Miami Beach. It was a far cry from his five dollar bill for "expenses" to attend the South Bend convention, and from his cubbyhole office on the West Side.

Reuther accomplished the great leap in membership of his West Side Local 174 by planning and winning a brief "sit-down" strike against the Kelsey-Hayes Wheel Company in Detroit. As spokesman for the West Side local and its workers at Kelsey-Hayes, Reuther approached the management to try to negotiate workers' grievances. The management would not talk with him, claiming that he did not work for them and could not represent their workers. Reuther and his lieutenants then planned a strike. They planned for a girl on the production line to feign a fainting spell. Thereupon other workers would turn off the power and stop the line. They would then run up and down the line shouting "Strike!" and try to persuade all the other workers to join in the sit-down or to leave the plant. Outside the plant near the gate the local would station a truck with a loudspeaker to keep the strikers inside informed of developments in the negotiations and to keep them up to date on tactics. The strike came off exactly as planned. For more than a week the strikers subsisted on food hoisted over the fence to them. At last Kelsey-Hayes gave in, recognized West Local 174 of the UAW as its workers' bargaining agent, and in the subsequent negotiations granted a minimum hourly wage of 75c, high for the industry. It was Reuther's first big success as a UAW officer.

But the successful sit-down strike in December, 1936, at Kelsey-Hayes was a relatively small one compared to strikes of that kind which soon swept through the automobile industry. By early 1937 sit-down strikes had become an epidemic. One carefully planned sit-down strike in Flint, Michigan, soon focused the attention of the whole nation, and presented the state of Michigan and the United States government with difficult and seemingly contradictory imperatives of preserving the peace and enforcing the law. After several months of great danger to the peace, barely skirted by strikers and government, General Motors Corporation agreed to a partial acquiescence to the UAW demands, and the strike ended. Although not a top leader of the UAW at this time, Walter "kept turning up and making his voice heard," as one old CIO militant recollects in his memoirs. As a board member, of course, Reuther participated in the strategy discussions. He and his brothers are credited with proposing the over-all strategy of the strike, which called for the selecting of limited but critically important targets within General Motors' complex production system. Both Victor and Roy Reuther were by now paid organizers for the UAW and were assigned to the campaign in various capacities. Roy went to Flint at the beginning to work with Robert Travis, the principal organizer assigned to the effort. Victor organized one of the smaller and supportive sit-down strikes in Anderson, Indiana, before returning to Flint and the main theatre of operations.

The strike against General Motors in Flint and elsewhere began in late December, 1936. Workers in the Fisher Body plant in Cleveland, Ohio, walked off the job and were numerous enough to close the plant in a conventional strike with pickets marching up and down in front of the gates. In Flint, Michigan, workers in Fisher Body No. 1 grew suspicious of the management's motives when they observed preparations for the removal of important dies from the plant. While there was still something in the plant to strike against, the workers sat down inside the plant and refused to leave. They made their move on December 30, 1936, days before the D-day planned by the UAW.

This sudden and major strike against General Motors apparently took John L. Lewis by surprise. The CIO leadership was about to start its big drive against the steel companies, and at first considered the troubles in Flint and elsewhere in the automobile industry as irritating diversions. But Lewis soon realized the importance of the automobile strikes and after only a moment's hesitation backed them unstintingly.

The seizure of private property by trespassers calling themselves strikers caused great anguish at General Motors and also troubled the American public in general. Although the besieged workers maintained exemplary discipline and damaged none of the property they occupied, the legal problem seemed peculiarly knotty. Editorial discussion of the sit-down problem occupied columns and columns of the mass media in 1937. In Flint a "back to work" movement sprang into existence, generously financed and advertised, and led by George E. Boyer, a local businessman and former paymaster for

35

Buick Motors. General Motors succeeded in getting an early court injunction from Judge Edward D. Black ordering the strikers to evacuate the plant. But CIO Counsel Lee Pressman, by merely scanning a list of General Motors stockholders on a hunch, discovered that Judge Black owned stock in General Motors to the amount of over $200,000. When the sheriff and fifty Flint policemen appeared at the gate of the occupied Fisher Body plant to serve the court order, they were met with only howls of laughter from the strikers. From that point nobody seemed determined to serve or enforce that court order. But the UAW did not succeed either in its propagandistic demand for the impeachment of Judge Black.

On January 11, 1937, a small body of policemen appeared at the gate of Fisher Body No. 2, one of the two occupied factories, to prevent food from being passed into the plant to the strikers. In the afternoon the management turned off the heat in the plant, something not previously done because of the company's reluctance to risk the freezing of plumbing and machinery. Exhorted by Victor Reuther from the UAW sound truck near the gate, a body of strikers then broke through the small police guard to retake the gate. Then fifty or more Flint policemen appeared in force to try to dislodge the strikers at the gate and to reimpose the siege of the strikers inside. The ensuing fracas has gone down in the annals of the UAW as the "Battle of the Running Bulls," or the "Battle of Bulls' Run." The UAW defenders of the gate and the strikers inside fought back against the policemen's clubs and tear gas with bricks, bottles, and automobile door hinges catapulted from windows with slingshots made from tire inner tubes. Finally the strikers turned the fire hoses in the plant against the police. Icy jets of high pressure water won the battle for the UAW, and the police retreated. All through the fray Victor Reuther and others on the sound truck kept up a continuous encouragement to the strikers. "We wanted peace. General Motors chose war. Give it to them!"

Governor Frank Murphy had no recourse but to call out the National Guard. The next day 1500 Guardsmen patrolled the streets of Flint. Spokesmen for General Motors and the Flint Alliance insisted they be used to dislodge the trespassers by force. Governor Murphy found himself in an impossible situation. If he did what seemed to be his legal duty he would only precipitate a bloody war, the outcome of which nobody could predict. Finally, on January 15, he worked out a temporary arrangement in painful negotiations with General Motors Vice President William Knudsen and the UAW "Strategy Board," on which Walter Reuther was serving. The Gen-

36

eral Motors plants would be vacated on Sunday, January 17. But before the arrangement could be carried out the UAW fell into possession of a telegram from Knudsen to George Boysen, the leader of the Flint Alliance. In the telegram Knudsen virtually promised the Alliance exclusive collective bargaining rights in General Motors plants. The strikers called foul, claimed a betrayal of the arrangement by General Motors. They refused to move out of the plants as scheduled on Sunday. But expecting a forceful dislodgement from the Fisher Body plant No. 1, they strengthened their base of operations by occupying a new factory, Chevrolet plant No. 4 in Flint. They accomplished the move after an elaborate feint at Chevrolet plant No. 1. General Motors spies were expected to learn of the bogus move and to report it to the management. The management took its elaborate defensive precautions at the wrong factory.

On January 29, Circuit Judge Paul V. Gadola issued a second injunction against the sit-down, ordering the strikers out of General Motors properties by 3:00 P.M., February 3. Governor Murphy hurriedly arranged a negotiation between Knudsen and John L. Lewis. The fateful day came. John L. Lewis promised ominously, as he arrived in Michigan for the talks, that he would join the strikers and let himself be the Guardsmen's first target if the order to use force were given. Governor Murphy delayed the seemingly inevitable use of force. The negotiations progressed agonizingly for more than a week after the court's deadline. Finally, on February 11, Lewis and General Motors announced a settlement. It was, in fact, only a partial victory for the UAW. They lost most of their specific demands for such things as a thirty-hour workweek or a uniform minimum wage. General Motors also agreed to accept the UAW as the bargaining agent for its workers, but only in the seventeen plants closed or occupied by the strikers. But within those limits the UAW could celebrate a considerable victory. If for only a limited time within only some plants, the UAW had forced the largest corporation in America to agree to collective bargaining.

Historians agree that the Flint strike constituted one of the great turning points in the history of the American labor movement. Persons participating in the epic events were to recall them lovingly for decades, down to the present day. The struggle spawned a whole folklore of song and anecdote within the labor movement.

Celebrating the battle at Fisher Body plant No. 2, the UAW sang:

> Oh, it was a jolly sight,
>   On that wintry, chilly night,

When the bulls came out
　　To throw us from the fort.
But with bruises, bumps and jolts,
　　From the storm of nuts and bolts,
They just turned about
　　And made a line for the port!

Of the sit-down tactic itself, the UAW sang:

When they tie the can to a union man,
　　Sit down! Sit down!
When the speedup comes, just twiddle your thumbs.
　　Sit down! Sit down!
When the boss won't talk, don't take a walk.
　　Sit down! Sit down!

In the months of the General Motors strike, and the months immediately after, the really impenetrable walls against unionization seemed breached. But the Ford Motor Company, parts of the steel industry, and even General Motors after its first concessions, continued to fight hard in the losing battle to resist the whole program of the CIO: routine, institutionalized, and industry-wide collective bargaining. The United States Steel Corporation, to almost everybody's surprise, capitulated to the Steel Workers Organizing Committee of the CIO in early 1937 without a strike. Perhaps U.S. Steel recognized presciently that an institutionalized relationship with what would soon be called "Big Labor" was not all that bad, that under labor contracts the whole bother of worker discipline and on-the-job management and seniority could be left to the union, and that higher wages, in an oligopolistic industry, could be easily passed on to the public as consumer. Or perhaps U.S. Steel capitulated simply to avoid costly labor troubles when the Depression seemed to be lifting and business improving and as the ominous breakdown of the peace in Europe and Asia promised good business. In the automobile industry, Chrysler Automobile Company suffered a few strategic sit-down strikes and surrendered to the UAW. In a word, the period from 1937 to 1940 saw evidences that the CIO had won its war but that the mopping up would be costly and violent.

Within the steel industry, those companies other than U.S. Steel—called "Little Steel"—tried to fight on, even bloodily as at the famous "Memorial Day Massacre" near the Republic Steel plant in East Chicago. But the decision in the Jones and Laughlin Steel Company case, coming in the midst of the "Little Steel" strike and upholding the constitutionality of the Wagner Act, took the spirit

38

out of that corporation's victory against the CIO, if only in the long run. Perhaps the celebration of victory within the CIO and UAW after the Flint strike was not wrong but only premature.

Henry Ford, in particular, was determined to resist to the bitter end, despite the momentum of the UAW in 1937, and despite the difficulties he would have more and more in keeping his resistance even technically legal in the face of the Wagner Act and rulings by the National Labor Relations Board. He did have the advantage of having been able to learn from the misfortunes of his competitors. He obviously would not be surprised by sit-down strikes or out-maneuvered because of bad intelligence. Harry Bennett, a former Navy bantamweight boxer, directed the Ford Service Bureau of 3,000 armed security guards, spies and undercover agents, and strike-breakers. It was allegedly the largest private army in the world. Henry Ford trusted Bennett implicitly, and only Henry Ford had the power in the peculiarly feudal and anachronistic organization of the Ford Motor Company to veto any actions by Bennett. So the Ford Service Bureau recruited a strange and motley battalion of ex-prize-fighters, proto-fascist bully boys from Michigan's little extremist political parties, ex-convicts, ex-policemen, and assorted Detroit underworld characters. It was a body made up of "tough sons-of-bitches," as Bennett characterized them, "but every one a gentle-man."

Flushed with its early 1937 victories, the UAW announced a drive to organize Ford workers. To begin, the UAW proposed to pass out leaflets at the Rouge plant. Sixty UAW organizers, forty of them women auxiliaries, stationed themselves on and near the pedestrian overpass that crossed a road from a large parking lot to the gates of the plant. The large number of women among the petitioners testi-fies to the intimidation of workers within the plant. Most of the women were wives whose husbands were sympathetic to the UAW but too fearful to be publicly identified. Walter Reuther and Richard Frankensteen led the contingent of petitioners, armed with what proved to be a futile permit from the Dearborn City Council.

The Ford Service Bureau turned this first probe of the Ford citadel by the UAW into a bloody rout. Before the brutalities had ended many UAW organizers, men and women, had suffered banged heads, bruised bodies, and broken bones. Reporters and cameramen, forewarned of impending trouble, came out in force but few of them escaped having their notes seized or their cameras smashed and their persons roughed up.

The "Battle of the Overpass," as it has come to be named in

UAW folklore and history, made Walter Reuther a nationally known name and face. He and Frankensteen were singled out for particularly severe beatings, and much of their punishment found its way onto film which somehow escaped the rough censorship on the site of battle. *Time* magazine, and newspapers outside Detroit, published the pictures. For this unfavorable publicity and Henry Luce's editorial comment that in the long run Henry Ford might have suffered more than Reuther or Frankensteen, Ford withdrew all advertisements from *Time, Life,* and *Fortune* for a whole year and a half.

Both Reuther and Frankensteen had climbed the stairs from the parking lot to the overpass, challenged by only one hostile questioner on the stairs. On the overpass several dozen men slouching nonchalantly at the railings paid no particular heed to Reuther and Frankensteen as they posed for news photographers and answered reporters' questions. Then three members of the Ford Service Bureau climbed the stairs and approached Reuther and Frankensteen. "This is private property. Get the hell off of here!" one of the three shouted. Immediately the idle men at the railings turned and rushed at Reuther and Frankensteen and began to pummel and kick them. Reuther tried merely to protect his head with his arms but was nevertheless beaten to the pavement and kicked savagely in the head. When he stumbled to his feet and staggered back down the stairs to the parking lot, the attackers followed him. They adjusted their gaits in almost a leisurely manner to his stumbles and continued their blows as Reuther tried to duck between parked cars. A group of women with leaflets to distribute, arriving on a streetcar, distracted the attackers. They left Reuther to run over to intercept the women.

Frankensteen tried to fight back—or at least push his attackers away—and he was overwhelmed, kicked and pushed down the stairs. One man kicked him in the groin. Another ground his heel into his stomach. When he rose to his feet, they pulled his coat up over his head and shoulders to immobilize him while they continued the beating.

After being left in the parking lot cinders by the men of the Ford Service Bureau, Reuther and Frankensteen managed to make it to the street and flag down a car being driven by a photographer from the Detroit *Times.* The photographer drove the two ghastly looking men to a physician's office for X-rays and treatment.

The beatings in the parking lot, however, continued. William Merriweather, who had accompanied a group of the women, suffered a serious and permanent injury. His back was broken, but he slithered out of the battle under a parked car. Many of the women were also beaten or manhandled violently. One, kicked in the stomach, vomited at the feet of a horrified clergyman who had come with the forewarned reporters to observe. He implored a nearby mounted policeman to intervene to protect the woman but without signal success.

Ford and his spokesmen staunchly denied any responsibility for the violence. W. J. Cameron, the honey-voiced editorialist on the Ford radio program, the Ford Sunday Evening Hour, told delegates to a convention meeting in Detroit that Ford workers had never rioted, that there had never been any disturbances at peaceful Ford plants. Harry Bennett claimed that he had instructed his Ford Service Bureau to honor the permit granted the UAW by the Dearborn City Council. He did allow, however, that certain "loyal Ford workers," incensed at the un-American agitation by the UAW, may have spontaneously attacked the organizers. It was a brazen effort on his part because certain of the attacking men in the news photographs that escaped the scene were easily identified as employees of Bennett's Ford Service Bureau.

The National Labor Relations Board conducted hearings soon after the event to determine whether Ford had been guilty of "unfair labor practices" under the terms of the Wagner Act. Walter Reuther testified as the first witness for the UAW. Over 150 other witnesses produced, before the investigation was done, about 3,000 pages of testimony. Louis J. Colombo, Jr., counsel for the Ford Motor Company, cross-examined Reuther exhaustively and tried by innuendo and choice of questions—whatever Reuther's responses might have been—to suggest that Reuther and the UAW were part of an un-American and revolutionary conspiracy. He presented a version of the "Vic and Wal" letter from Russia, as we have seen above. He asked Reuther questions about his views on private property and revolution without detailing what relevancy the views, whatever they might have been, would have to the matter being investigated.[2]

Q. You went to Russia?
A. That is correct?

Q. You and your brother were in Russia?
A. Well, I have already told you that. We worked there.

Q. You both worked in factories in Russia?
A. That is correct.

41

Q. And you went over there to study their system of government, didn't you?
A. I studied their system the same as I studied the system of Germany, Italy, and Japan.

Q. I am not talking about that.
A. You asked me why I went there.

Q. One of the purposes of going there was to study the Soviet system of government?
A. The purpose—

Q. Please answer the question. Was it?
A. We went to Russia to study conditions there the same as we did in Germany.

Q. The Russian system of government?
A. No, we didn't. We went there to study conditions.

Q. What conditions: political conditions and economic conditions?
A. Social and economic conditions.

Q. In other words, the Russian—the political, the social, and the economic conditions under the Soviet Union, is that not right?
A. We went there to study, as I said before, the social conditions of Russia as we did in other countries.

Q. Under the Soviet system?
A. Naturally, it would be the Soviet system.

Q. You also studied the method they used to start riots—?
A. I never saw any riots started in Russia.

Q. All right. Did you study the Russian method of revolution?
A. I didn't. I worked there in a factory as a technician.

Q. Are you a Communist?
A. I am not, never have been.

Q. You never have been a Communist and you are not a Communist now?
A. That is correct.

Q. Do you have any respect for private property?
A. I do.

Q. Do you respect private property?
A. I do.

Q. Are you a member of the CIO?
A. I am.

Q. And the UAW?
A. I am.

Q. How many Communists belong to the CIO?
A. I am in no position to tell you that.

Q. How many Communists are there in the UAW?
A. I can't answer that either.

The National Labor Relations Board, after hours of this somewhat time-killing examination and cross-examination, found the Ford Motor Company at fault. "The testimony concerning the events on the overpass establishes that the attack upon the union group was vicious and unnecessarily brutal, particularly in view of the fact that no resistance was offered by those attacked. Reuther and Frankensteen were singled out for particular attention and given terrific beatings. . . ."

Three months after this losing skirmish, the UAW resumed the attack. Reuther, in the middle of a factional fight within the UAW, was ordered out of the fray by the executive board. But a thousand husky and grim-faced automobile workers passed out leaflets in August undisturbed. Agents of the Ford Service Bureau merely stood and watched. But the Dearborn City Council predictably rescinded its permit and in its stead passed an ordinance prohibiting the passing out of leaflets in "congested areas." Through the rest of 1937 the police made over a thousand arrests for violation of the ordinance. To avoid a court appeal and a test of the constitutionality of the ordinance, the authorities held prisoners only the minimum time allowable without charges and the possibility of writs of habeas corpus and then released them. The arrests, however, succeeded in hampering the UAW's drive.

In the meantime, the intimidation of workers inside Ford plants continued unabated. However favorable their private opinions might have been toward the UAW, few workers dared become open advocates of unionization. From 1937 to 1940 the National Labor Relations Board judged Ford Motor Company guilty of violations of the Wagner Act in nine of its plants. In a few places—particularly the Ford plant in Dallas, Texas—the testimony before the NLRB describes a virtual reign of terror, enforced by beatings with blackjacks and even shootings. The heated factional dispute within the UAW, which we shall discuss in the next chapter, slowed the drive even though the UAW never completely abandoned the fight.

In 1940 the tide began to turn. The UAW began to receive massive support from the CIO, and the entire labor movement in Detroit began to cooperate with the organizational drive. Even milk wagon drivers, given the names of Ford workers on their routes, began to do missionary work for the UAW by trying to persuade the workers to come out and declare their interest in the union. The NLRB also ordered the company to rehire twenty-two workers fired from the Rouge plant and to give the usual retroactive wage payments. Henry Ford, of course, appealed the decision to the federal courts. The Supreme Court upheld the NLRB by refusing to hear the case, and the rebuff to Ford reacted to the benefit of the UAW. Thousands of workers began to join the UAW and to wear their buttons to work openly. In October, 1940, Justice of the Peace Lila Neuenfelt of Dearborn declared the ordinance prohibiting the distribution of leaflets to be unconstitutional. A Michigan court upheld her ruling. By January, 1941, the UAW was proselytizing openly around the gates of Ford plants and signing up members virtually under the scowls of Harry Bennett's guards. When in February, 1941, the twenty-two reinstated men went back to work, Ford had obviously lost his last opportunity to delay unionization by delaying tactics in the courts.

In early 1941, a veritable epidemic of strikes began to cripple production in Ford plants all over the country. On December 30, 1940, for example, over a thousand men in the tool and die department of the Rouge plant left their jobs. When they returned to work, however, they discovered that their personally owned tools which they had left in the plant had been destroyed by the Ford Service Bureau in their absence.

For February, 1941, the UAW announced a big, formal strike against the Rouge, Highland, and Lincoln plants of the Ford Motor Company. In March and April the strike had spread to Ford facilities all over the country. At this juncture, Homer Martin, the president of the UAW from 1936 to 1939 and thereafter the leader of a small rival UAW affiliated with the AFL, threatened a "back to work" movement. His shock troops were hundreds of Negro workers stranded in some of the struck plants and hundreds of others recruited from the unemployed. His maneuver threatened not so much a jurisdictional labor struggle between the CIO and the AFL as it did a race riot. Prominent Negro leaders, nationally and from Michigan, hurriedly tried to educate their communities as to what was afoot and the dangers implicit in Martin's tactic. Frightened Negro workers in the Ford plants, who had been recruited by Martin's rump UAW and then "protected" by Harry Bennett, were soon besieged by angry pickets on all the roads leading to the factories. Walter White, head of the National Association for the Advancement of Colored People, and other nóted leaders, exhorted the workers in the plants from sound trucks to leave. The UAW promised them safe passage through the pickets. Even the AFL unions in Detroit repudiated Martin, calling him a strike-breaker rather than a bona fide labor leader. The "back to work" movement, worked out in apparent collusion between Harry Bennett and Homer Martin, fortunately withered.

On April 10, 1941, the Ford Motor Company accepted a compromise settlement suggested by the Governor of Michigan. The strike ended. In May, the NLRB conducted a representational election among Ford workers. The UAW won 58,000 out of the 80,000 votes cast. Those voting for no union at all came to fewer than 3% of the total. Homer Martin's little rump UAW received about a fourth of the vote. The election returns would seem to belie that reiterated burden of Ford propaganda that his workers wanted no unions at all and were resentful of the intimidation by the UAW subversives and "Communists." Bennett called the election "a great victory for the Communist Party, Governor Van Wagoner and the National Labor Relations Board," implying, confusedly perhaps, that there might be some kind of identity between the putative victors.

Harry Bennett may have felt initially betrayed, but upon orders from Ford he now decided to make the best of the situation. In negotiations with the UAW he offered the best contract that any CIO union to that date had obtained. Ford agreed to a full union program, the exclusive union shop, the dues check off, grievance-settling arrangements, seniority, time-and-a-half for overtime, and premium time for night work. Within the next year the UAW negotiated $52,000,000 in additional wages for its Ford workers.

In 1948, after enactment of the Taft-Hartley Act, Ford workers had another opportunity to vote in an NLRB election on the question of whether they wished to keep the UAW union shop. Of 98,000 eligible voters, over 90,000 voted even though the polling places were inconveniently located outside the plants. Almost all of the 90,000 voted to continue the UAW representation.

The years from 1936 to 1940 saw the CIO—and the UAW—make

a revolution. For the first time in American history millions of workers organized themselves into industrial unions and began to make institutionalized, legally protected collective bargaining an ordinary part of American life. The historical magnitude of the change is difficult to imagine for generations already come to maturity, who consequently accept its ordinariness. The old days of the Molly Maguires, the Homestead strike, the IWW, that whole era in our civilization before 1940 is, of course, "pre-revolutionary." During that long era of struggle the labor movement was the cutting edge of equalitarianism, of social reform, of social reconstruction, of hope. The CIO—and the UAW—was the New Left, the Vietnam protest, the Civil Rights revolution of its day—and somehow the comparison vaguely cheapens the CIO. Walter Reuther began to emerge as a leader of this revolution as early as the 1936 South Bend convention of the UAW. By the time of the "Battle of the Overpass" a year later he had become one of its most visible leaders.

CHAPTER FOUR

Homer Martin, the first president chosen by the UAW for itself, had once been nicknamed the "Leaping Parson." Born in the coal mining area of Southern Illinois and ordained as a Baptist minister at the age of nineteen after a few years in a Kansas City seminary, he had, as a hobby, won all the competitions in the hop, skip, and jump track event. He was named to the United States track team for the 1924 Olympic Games. At the last moment he found himself unable to go, and his athletic career ended quietly afterwards. In the early Depression years he became the minister of a Baptist church in a small town on the outskirts of Kansas City. His parishioners, mostly automobile workers, came to involve him more and more in their troubles. When he began to offer unwanted advice to the employers in the Kansas City automobile plants, some of his more conservative and affluent parishioners asked him to leave. So, in 1934, Martin took a job in Kansas City as an automobile worker, and joined the recently organized automobile union. His forensic skills as a fundamentalist Baptist minister lifted him quickly into prominence in the new union. Events were soon to trip Martin up and demonstrate that fervent preaching may have been his only real qualification for leadership. But in the early days of the UAW such a skill was not unimportant, especially in a union composed largely of Southern and Appalachian workers. In 1935 the AFL leaders appointed him vice-president of the UAW. The following year, as we have seen, delegates to the South Bend convention elected him president.

Anecdotes concerning his administrative ineptitude abound. During the planning stage of the Flint strike Martin disclosed to one of the board members a telegram he was about to send to all the UAW locals in the country, ordering them out on strike. All the discussions in the board meetings, by Reuther and the others, on the desirability of striking only selected strategic plants in the complex General Motors structure had apparently missed him or left him unconvinced. When the board members remonstrated with Martin that his telegram would be a disaster, that the UAW was simply not strong enough for such broad action, Martin explained that he did not really mean the telegram to be implemented. He intended to cancel it at the last minute. He only proposed to send it as a means of frightening General Motors. It took the intervention of an aide of John L. Lewis to persuade Martin not to go through with his plan.

After the Flint strike and the only partial victory over General Motors, the automobile plants became arenas of subtle and bitter guerilla warfare. Management fulfilled only the letter of its agreements, and that they did reluctantly. Grievance-settling machinery was primitive. The workers rankled under the continuing boredom and nervousness of speed-ups and under the continued tyranny of foremen, made worse by a sense of disillusionment after having apparently won a strike. General Motors plants averaged almost a strike a day through the remainder of 1937, small wildcat protests indicative of the tensions and unresolved problems. Martin worked himself into an embarrassing position with both his own union and management when he embarked upon negotiations to deal with the problem of wildcat strikes, and such breaches of contract by the union. He agreed too readily to a management request for the right to disciplinary action. Militant shop stewards, meeting in Detroit, took President Martin to task for the "sell out" and repudiated his agreement. Martin then rescinded the agreement, to the accompanying charges of bad faith by management.

Dissatisfaction with Martin within the union began to mount almost immediately after his election. Martin sensed it and tried increasingly to use the constitutional—and even extra-constitu-

47

tional—powers of his office to shore up his failing political position in the union. He grew very suspicious, with good cause, of the motives of many of the new and vigorous leaders in the union who had come into national prominence as a result of the Flint strike. He ordered the largest local union in the UAW, in Detroit, broken up so as to disperse a rival's constituency and his possible base of delegate strength at the next convention. He transferred and dismissed organizers who roused his suspicions, including Roy and Victor Reuther. He defended his arbitrary suspensions by claiming that the victims of his action were agents of "outside organizations," by which he meant the Communist Party and the Socialist Party. He also hurriedly chartered many new locals as a means of garnering delegates for himself at the next convention of the union.

An opposition faction began to take form in the UAW, calling itself the "Unity" caucus. Wyndham Mortimer, the leader of the Cleveland strike in 1937 and supposedly close to the Communist Party, and the Reuthers with their unconcealed connections to the Socialist Party, and several other politically unaffiliated militants, led the new faction. Martin, with Frankensteen as his principal ally, organized a "Progressive" caucus. The tension and rivalry within the union increased, although it did not seem to hamper, peculiarly enough, the phenomenal growth of the union throughout the industry. Both "Progressive" and "Unity" caucuses, of course, looked ahead to the forthcoming convention of the UAW scheduled for August, 1937. The Progressive caucus convened in pre-convention strategy meetings in South Bend, Indiana. The Unity caucus met for the same purposes in Toledo, Ohio.

Over a thousand delegates arrived in Milwaukee, Wisconsin, in August for the convention, most of them aligned with one or the other of the two caucuses. When Martin made his first appearance at the beginning of the convention his delegates gave him a noisy standing ovation that lasted ninety minutes. Even delegates in the Unity caucus, after a few minutes of awkward non-participation, rose to join soberly in the demonstration.

The Progressives made the first important proposal, a plan to reduce the representation of the larger locals, such as Reuther's, and to increase greatly the representation of the numerous small locals. Because Unity caucus strength came principally from the large locals, Martin's motives seemed transparent to the convention. Reuther made an impassioned speech against the motion and its "anti-democratic" tendency. The motion did not carry. The Unity caucus then proposed that pre-convention meetings such as those held at

South Bend and Toledo be prohibited. The convention tabled the motion. Frankensteen spoke against the motion and presented the views of Martin, himself, and the Progressives. He said such meetings were, alas, necessary. If prohibited, then only the "outsiders" would in fact have them and derive all the advantages from them. Again, by "outsiders" he alluded to Communists and Socialists.

The Martin administration then presented a centralizing plan to limit some of the embarrassing autonomy of the locals in such matters as wildcat strikes and to give the president vastly augmented disciplinary powers. John L. Lewis had, in fact, drafted the plan because he was disturbed by the rash of wildcat strikes. Although Reuther and others in the Unity caucus spoke vigorously against the proposal, the convention eventually adopted its essential parts with the "compromise" benevolently "suggested" to the faction-ridden UAW by John L. Lewis, Sidney Hillman, and other CIO leaders. Lewis and his lieutenants had come to Milwaukee to try to put the UAW back on its feet. They conferred and negotiated and argued vigorously off the floor of the convention with both factions.

Besides the granting of more presidential disciplinary powers to Martin, the convention adopted a general plan to try to contain the factional dispute. Martin was to continue as president, and all the incumbent vice-presidents—including Mortimer of the Unity caucus—would also continue in office. Two new vice-presidents were named, Frankensteen and R. J. Thomas. The executive board, upon which Reuther sat, should be expanded from twelve members to seventeen. The "compromise" benefited mostly the Martin administration and the Progressive caucus, although Reuther, Mortimer, and the other Unity caucus leaders at least kept their seats on the executive board. The Unity caucus lost most clearly in the provisions granting new powers to President Martin, and in the new provision that conventions would be held only every other year.

When Martin began to attack the opposition Unity caucus seeking to unseat him as "outsiders" who represented the interests of the Communist Party, he raised the curtain on a drama that was to bemuse the UAW for at least the next decade. The same drama was to preoccupy the whole CIO, and indeed the whole country, by the late 1940's. Reuther, as we shall see, emerged from the decade of complicated factional dispute as president of the UAW. He also emerged as a national leader of liberal anti-Communism in an era when anti-Communism, from right to left, became the virtual orthodoxy in American political life. Obviously some strange and complicated things must have happened, inside and outside the UAW, from

1937, when Reuther and the Socialists were allied with Communists in the Unity caucus, and 1946 and 1947, when Reuther emerged as a national hero of anti-Communism. It is not out of place to try to sketch this larger context of the struggles within the UAW during the rise of Reuther.

As we have already related, young Walter Reuther came to Detroit from Wheeling, West Virginia, and then travelled to Russia, during that "Third Period" of the Communist "line." Communists from 1928 to the mid-1930's took the position that the historic revolutionary moment had again arrived, just as in 1917 and 1918. Only Communists had the proper understanding of the times and knew how to lead the working class into and through the imminent revolutionary crisis. As during the period of the First World War, the Socialists—and other assorted "bourgeois" liberals and radicals—would only lose their nerve, mislead the masses, and betray the revolution again as they had in 1914. Consequently, liberals, radicals, and Socialists outside the discipline of the Communist Party constituted the worst danger to the working class. In fact, they were really "Social Fascists," because they would betray the workers, in the moment of great opportunity, to Fascism, that last gasp of a dying capitalism trying to save itself with dictatorship.

In a word, Walter and Victor Reuther as Socialists were officially part of the Communist movement's worst enemy as they labored conscientiously in the Gorki automobile plant. In all likelihood their Russian hosts—and their American Communist friend, John Rushton—accepted their help in the same spirit that they accepted Henry Ford's offer of Model A dies. Reuther's "ecumenical"—as we have called it—willingness to include Communists within his Socialism was really of little interest to the Communists.

By 1936—even by 1935—it became increasingly obvious to Joseph Stalin and to other Comintern leaders that the "line" of the Third Period had misfired. It did not appear to be working out so simply, as Communists had said in 1932 and 1933, that "After Hitler, Us!" In Germany and around the world the revolution again had not come. Instead, Fascism in Europe seemed a frighteningly permanent threat to the Soviet Union. As a consequence of the new evaluation, the Comintern shifted its line. By the time in 1936 when Socialists and Communists in France entered into a formal coalition under Leon Blum to form a "Popular Front" government, the same tactics of coalition had become the international line. Now all peace-loving and democratic forces were to be welcomed as allies of the Communists. In the early New Deal years, coinciding with the

Third Period line, American Communists had attacked Franklin D. Roosevelt as a lackey of the DuPonts, and his New Deal as Fascism. By the election of 1936, the American Communist Party hardly bothered to campaign for Earl Browder, its own official candidate for the presidency. Even Earl Browder made it "no secret" that he himself was really for Roosevelt. Thus the "Popular Front" came to America.

As Marxists who viewed the working class under capitalism as the instrument of the coming revolution, Communists had an obvious interest in the labor movement. After the supposedly revolutionary crisis of the First World War had passed, the young American Communist Party retreated into a policy of attaching itself—and hopefully of influencing—the existing labor movement. Then in the Third Period after 1928 the Party abandoned its policy of parasitic attachment to the AFL and boldly formed its own revolutionary "dual" unions. It also attacked the AFL—as well as Socialists, New Dealers, and the non-Communist Left, as we have seen—as "Social Fascists." By the mid-1930's, however, they began to discard their disruptive but ineffectual "dual" unions and, as part of the United or Popular Front line, to return to the AFL. Such was the state of relative indecision and translation that prevailed when John L. Lewis began in 1935 to organize his Committee of Industrial Organization.

John L. Lewis, as chief of the United Mine Workers, had never been a hero of the Communists. But the Popular Front, together with Lewis' need for dedicated and experienced organizers, produced an enthusiastic marriage of the Communist Party and the early CIO. Lewis discovered in his early drives against the steel, rubber, automobile, chemical, and electrical industries that he simply did not have enough experienced organizers from his United Mine Workers to go around. He therefore welcomed the many volunteers with Communist connections without asking too many questions. It has been claimed, with some cogency, that John L. Lewis, a political and economic conservative and a Republican Party supporter in the main, was one of the few men who ever succeeded in "duping" Communists rather than vice versa. Certainly many Communist activists and skilled organizers figured prominently in the early history of the CIO, and with at least the tacit blessing of Lewis.

After three or more years of Popular Front, of trying to rally the political middle and left in a grand alliance against Fascism, Stalin in August, 1939, startled the world with a non-aggression friendship pact with Hitler's Germany. This was a complete reversal of policy which he had negotiated without even forewarning Communists around the world of the impending dramatic change. Obviously Stalin had made a cynical, realistic bargain. He could have accepted the last minute and half-hearted overtures of the French and British to join them in trying to deter Hitler, which he knew might very well put him into a war with Germany in a matter of weeks or days. Or he could accept Hitler's offer, which would at least mean no immediate war and the further possibility of being the neutral beneficiary of any long war that came about between Germany and the Western powers. In the suspicious mind of Stalin, had not England and France tried to direct Hitler eastward against him in 1938 at the Munich agreement, or "Appeasement"? He was only cleverly turning the tables on England and France and directing Hitler westward.

Between August, 1939, and June, 1941, when Hitler broke his treaty with Stalin and invaded Russia, the international Communist line adopted the view that the Second World War was merely an imperialist struggle from which Communists and "progressives" in all countries should disengage. In the United States the Communist Party became vociferously isolationist. Communists picketed the White House carrying banners proclaiming Roosevelt to be a warmonger and that the "Yanks aren't coming!"

In June, 1941, six months before Pearl Harbor, the German armies invaded the Soviet Union. The Communist line, of course, changed immediately and dramatically. Discomfited pickets around the White House did not know what to do immediately when the news broke. Within a day, however, the Second World War became a "Peoples' War" and American Communists became ardent interventionists. After Pearl Harbor they became virtual super-patriots and supporters of the American war effort. Within the labor unions they sometimes came to jettison even traditional trade unionist interests and to advocate such things as piece work and incentive pay plans to stimulate war production.

Obviously none of these increasingly sycophantic policy changes by American Communists went unnoticed in the labor movement, and in the UAW. They served to give great credibility, as we shall see, to the charges by the anti-Communist Left after the war—for which Reuther became a national spokesman and leader—that Communists were merely the obsequious tools of the foreign policy of an unfriendly nation.

But it is really not all that simple. Even the Communists included in their ranks a wide range of persons and personalities and personal histories. Villains are never, or rarely, unequivocal villains in history.

In the heat of battle the would-be heroes also take some of the undesirable attributes of the villains. And as one militant CIO editor and alleged Communist of those days has said in his recent thoughtful memoirs, it is the "good guys" like Walter Reuther of the Cold War era who won the war and have written all the standard histories.[1] Certainly the number of actual Communists in the UAW constituted a minute minority of the membership, perhaps only 500 in a total membership of more than half a million. None of the factional leaders in the UAW reputedly in the "Communist camp"— George Addes or R. J. Thomas, for example—were themselves Communists. At best their political power in the UAW rested in constituencies or big locals led by strategically placed Communists. In order not to prejudge the conflict too egregiously by using the categories of the winners we shall sometimes refer to the Communist-controlled faction in the UAW as "Communist."

After the 1937 convention of the UAW and the imposed "compromise" by the CIO leaders, the conflict did not subside. But the two factions supporting and opposing Martin began to change and shift. Martin continued to suspend and discharge organizers and officials he disliked under the new powers granted him by the 1937 convention. "How Homer liked to suspend people," mused one CIO historian years later. Martin also interfered with the newspapers of dissident locals, censoring news stories and editorial positions. He appointed his ally, Frankensteen, to the post of "Assistant President," although there was no such constitutional post.

Martin's ineptitude as a factional politician, as well as his already recognized inadequacies as an executive, revealed themselves when he lost even his principal ally on the executive board, Frankensteen, and when he failed completely to take account or advantage of a rift which began to appear in 1938 between Reuther and the "Communists" in the Unity caucus. In this Popular Front period, as we have seen, the Communists cultivated non-Communist radicals and liberals in the interests of their coalition strategy. They wooed the Reuther brothers, in particular, because of their reputed friendship toward the Soviet Union and because of Walter's and Victor's actual residence in the Socialist fatherland. The marriage of convenience called the Unity caucus had obviously sprung from such propinquity and opportunity. Some leaders of the Socialist Party criticized the Reuthers from the beginning for their lack of sophistication in their alliance with the Communists and "Communists."

In 1937, during the height of the factional dispute, several prominent American Communist Party leaders—Earl Browder and Louis

Budenz, for example—approached Walter Reuther with offers of a more intimate alliance if he were to join the Party. In exchange, the Communists could assure Reuther the presidency of the UAW as their man. Reuther turned down the offer. By early 1938 he began to notice a cooling toward him in the Unity caucus alliance, a withholding of support by the Communists. In Michigan he lost his race for an important CIO state office because of the switch of Communist Party support to another candidate.

Strange things also began to happen on the executive board of the UAW. Frankensteen abandoned Homer Martin and the Progressive caucus and came out in opposition to his former allies. In June, 1938, Martin suspended from office Frankensteen and four other members of the executive board, including George Addes and Wyndham Mortimer of the Unity caucus. Martin claimed to be foiling a Communist conspiracy within the UAW. The suspended board members countered with a charge of conspiracy by a small splinter group of Communists, followers of Jay Lovestone who had "captured" Homer Martin. In support of the counter-charge, Addes and Mortimer published letters pilfered from Lovestone which more or less substantiated it. Lovestone, in turn, charged that Russian Secret Police agents had stolen the letters from him. In this more and more Byzantine conflict the expelled leaders appealed directly to the national CIO for a hearing. John L. Lewis agreed to review the case. Martin then ineptly lost much of his support from the rank and file by denouncing the almost sacrosanct figure of John L. Lewis. "I will not turn over the international UAW to John L. Lewis," he blustered. When Philip Murray and Sidney Hillman proposed a virtual receivership by the CIO of the UAW—a severe limitation of Martin's presidential powers and a reinstating of the expelled leaders—Martin had little popular support within the union upon which to base resistance. All parties accepted another CIO-imposed "compromise."

To retrieve his sagging prestige Martin then entered into almost private and secret negotiations with Henry Ford, operating apparently on the naive assumption that Ford was ignorant of conditions in his own factories and that if he knew of them he would agree to unionization. The talks came to naught, except to produce rumors throughout the union that Martin was "selling-out" the UAW to Ford. At this point another Martin supporter on the executive board deserted him. R. J. Thomas, a bluff and apolitical "pure and simple" unionist, accused Martin of discussing with Ford in the course of their talks appropriate ways to separate the UAW from the CIO.

Since the 1936 South Bend convention the opinion in the UAW had been solidly in favor of the CIO, and the charges of R. J. Thomas probably damaged Martin more than anything he had yet done or been accused of doing.

In January, 1939, the executive board voted to call another convention of the UAW, obviously to deal with the mounting organizational problems and to get rid of Martin. Because he knew the mind of his board Martin opposed the motion. He summarily suspended fifteen of the twenty-four board members. In the ensuing hullabaloo he became almost incommunicado and inaccessible, appearing only in the midst of burly body guards, never answering his telephone, always "not in" when people called on him. Thus, almost completely isolated and holding onto power by only a few remaining threads, he announced a UAW convention of his own. It was clear he intended to take the UAW out of the CIO on his own initiative. In March, 1939, therefore, *two* conventions of the UAW convened. Delegates representing about 60,000 Martin supporters appeared in Detroit. Martin, speaking to them, received another thundering sixty-minute ovation. His convention then proceeded to vote the UAW out of the CIO and into the AFL. Most of the UAW, however, sent delegates to the convention called by the executive board in Cleveland, Ohio.

Even with Martin gone, the convention in Cleveland experienced no sudden peace. The "Communists," obviously riding high and with their whole opposition gone or in disarray, nominated a "sure thing" slate of candidates led by George Addes and Frankensteen. The latter's break with Martin thus might seem adequately explained. At this point the Reuther faction—if it could be called that yet—of Socialists, former Socialists, and apolitical trade unionists led by R. J. Thomas, had little chance of blocking the "Communist" steamroller. But again Philip Murray and Sidney Hillman from the national CIO offices intervened. In conferences and meetings off the floor of the convention they told the Addes faction leaders quite explicitly not to press on to the victory their delegate strength made quite possible. Bowing to this prestigious intervention, the "Communists" and the Reuther forces agreed to support a compromise candidate on whom both could agree, at least for the moment. R. J. Thomas was elected president.

Thomas remained president through the Second World War and into 1946. The factions during the war years fluctuated but in the main remained in balance, an equilibrium from which Thomas benefited. As Reuther's faction grew in prestige and power during the

55

war—and Reuther had become by far the best known leader of the UAW long before he attained the presidency—the Addes faction swung its support behind Thomas to keep him in office and to check Reuther. Thomas was a large and amiable man, a "pork chopper," interested primarily in the bread and butter issues of unionism. He tended to become irritated with "intellectuals" such as Reuther. Completely approachable, tobacco-chewing, poker-playing, he developed a tremendously loyal following in the union and was hardly alert to, or perhaps interested in, the alleged way in which the Addes faction, or "Communists," came to "capture" him.

As the United States began to rearm during 1940 and 1941, and after Pearl Harbor became totally involved in the war, the UAW factional conflict came to revolve around issues related to the war. The UAW, of course, made a patriotic "no strike" pledge after Pearl Harbor which by 1943 and 1944 began to trouble and irritate thousands of automobile workers caught in the wartime, only partially controlled, inflation. The corporations seemed protected against the inflationary pressures by cost-plus contracts while labor shouldered more than its share of the burden without any chance of redress because of the pledge. At the Buffalo, New York, convention of the UAW in 1943, the Thomas-Addes leadership even proposed an "incentive pay," or piecework, plan for the automobile industry in order to stimulate war production. Such schemes were ordinarily anathema to trade unionists because they always led to speed-ups and to upward-creeping production quotas for even minimal pay. Reuther spoke vigorously against the plan. Cynical delegates poked fun at the sudden patriotism of the "Communist" sponsors of the plan by waving little American flags whenever Addes or another of its proponents spoke. Or they sang the following song:

> Who are the boys who take their orders
> Straight from the office of Joe Sta-leen?
> No one else but the gruesome twosome,
> George F. Addes and Frankensteen.
>
> Who are the boys that fight for piecework,
> To make the worker a machine?
> No one else but the gruesome twosome,
> George F. Addes and Frankensteen.

Delegates in opposition to the "Communist" leadership opened an attack on the "no strike" pledge when its continuation came up on the floor of the convention for discussion. The angry delegates dilated on the guaranteed profits of the corporations and on the stupidity of the UAW leadership in relinquishing its only weapon as a labor union, the strike. Reuther straddled this explosive issue, supporting the "no strike" pledge, helping it withstand this assault, but as part of a larger program of spreading the sacrifices. Reuther's plan came to naught in the practical politics of the convention, and in effect he supported the administration in retaining the pledge.

In 1944 a "Rank and File" caucus, independent of both the Reuther and the "Communist" faction, appeared in sudden strength at the UAW convention. Its brief strength for a time ate into Reuther's support. The issue in contention again was the "no strike" pledge. Nat Ganley, a convention "whip" for the Thomas-Addes leadership, proposed a continuation of the pledge. He won support, ironically, from most of the politically conservative and "patriotic" delegates for this program of the "Communists." Reuther again straddled the issue by proposing a continuation of the pledge only in those plants doing war contract work. The Rank and File faction, of course, argued vehemently for its outright repeal. In the convention vote the Rank and File faction garnered 37% of the vote, enough to prevent any of the three positions on the no strike pledge from winning. At this point a disingenuous delegate rose to ask whether the vote meant that the UAW had *no* official position any more on wartime strikes, whether the locals were now free to do whatever they wished. In some embarrassment the Reuther delegates and the Thomas-Addes delegates came together to vote in a simple continuation of the no strike pledge. In a subsequent referendum of the membership the Rank and File caucus again won a surprising 35% of the vote.

As the war came to an end in 1945 and the period of reconversion to peacetime production began, Reuther became the leader and the principal strategist of a bitter strike against General Motors. The strike catapulted him into national fame, and he even became a controversial figure among his own labor leaders within the CIO. At any rate, by 1946 he considered his own position and his political "machine" in the UAW strong enough to make his bid for the presidency against R. J. Thomas and the "Communist" faction. He began an ardent "educational" campaign within the union with the general motto: "Against Outside Interference." The interference he had in mind was, of course, the Communist Party. Within all the locals where his troops operated he hammered away at the strictly union, the "pork chop," disadvantages of Communist influence within the UAW. He made much of the Communist Party's wild

57

shifts in policy in 1939 and 1941 and how these extraneous "political" interests had hurt the union in material ways. He explained the pointless strikes against preparedness by some Communist-dominated locals in 1940 and early 1941, and the sacrifices of basic workers' interests in the wartime "incentive pay" plan. In Detroit and other cities he organized "seminars" for his factional leaders, shop stewards, organizers, and local officials. In these meetings the education progressed at a reputedly higher level of sophistication, taking into account the history of the Left, the issues in the developing Cold War, and the general social and political role of the labor movement.

In this drive for the presidency Reuther counted on the support of ordinary political conservatives in the union who would be predisposed to "anti-Communism"; of the newly organized Association of Catholic Trade Unionists, also predisposed to anti-Communism; and of various radical and liberal anti-Communist intellectuals who, like himself, were an increasingly important phenomenon in American political life, in and out of the labor movement. Other members were obviously attracted to the Reuther campaign simply because he was energetic, original, and full of new ideas that seemed to be coming from no other leaders.

In the practical politics of the campaign Reuther had most of the advantages. The Thomas-Addes leadership had supported piecework and incentive pay during the war, and Reuther obviously had a much better record on that issue to which he could point with pride. The Thomas-Addes faction had carped at and criticized Reuther's leadership in the recent General Motors strike and had supported what Reuther interpreted as the sabotage of the strike by other Communist-dominated unions in the CIO. The Thomas-Addes faction considered Reuther's energetic "education" in the locals to be "red baiting," an instinctive response from the old days of 1935 and 1937, which by 1946 seemed less and less responsive to a real question to more and more UAW members. In March, 1946, at the Atlantic City convention Reuther won the presidency by a narrow margin of votes. To his dismay he found himself president with an executive board still controlled by the Thomas-Addes faction.

The factional struggle did not subside but, if anything, grew more heated. Jockeying for power in the locals, as well as on the executive board, became the full-time activity for many union leaders. Then, in the spring of 1947, the opposition to Reuther made its fateful blunder. A small Farm Equipment Workers union in the CIO often

58

came into jurisdictional conflict with the UAW. The Thomas-Addes faction, in control of the executive board of the UAW, proposed a merger. Because "unity" in the labor movement is almost an unarguable good, the advocates of the merger thought themselves unassailable. Reuther immediately sensed his danger. The Farm Equipment Workers union was "Communist"-led. The envisioned merger would tremendously augment the Thomas-Addes factional strength at conventions, because the Farm Equipment Workers were to have semi-autonomous status with consequent gross over-representation at conventions.

Reuther and his supporters began another furious "educational" campaign in advance of the referendum on the merger question. Reuther even held public debates on the plan, including a debate with George Addes himself before about 2500 UAW organizers and officials in Detroit. Again Reuther succeeded in explicating the political motives behind the "unity" proposal. The merger proposal lost by a two to one vote of the UAW membership.

When in 1947 the UAW assembled again in Atlantic City, Reuther had swept all before him. Even Philip Murray of the CIO jumped unequivocally on the Reuther bandwagon. At the 1946 convention he had scarcely concealed his real personal preference for R. J. Thomas over Reuther. Reuther was re-elected, and he won control also of the executive board. The Thomas-Addes forces were routed. The press reported the results of this convention as a "swing to the right," although Reuther and his many liberal and radical anti-Communist supporters were pained by that characterization.[2]

Securely in charge after 1947, Reuther quickly purged the UAW of its most obvious Communist and "Communist" elements. He discharged, for example, about a hundred staff members. George Addes left the UAW and the labor movement to open a night club. R. J. Thomas left the UAW to take a minor job with the national offices of the CIO. Reuther had at last arrived. His political position was never seriously threatened within the UAW from that summer of 1947 to his death in 1970.

CHAPTER FIVE

Walter Reuther became a man of power and historical importance years before he reached the presidency of the United Automobile Workers in 1946. When he early attained that peculiar pinnacle of fame to which Americans give the name "celebrity," in the spring of 1937, it was for his youthful audacity and his suspected radicalism. Then, during those feverish months of public opinion change and military preparedness, between the fall of France in the summer of 1940 and the Pearl Harbor attack at the end of 1941, he became known as an "idea man," an "intellectual" in the labor movement. After the war, at the height of his early career, he continued to combine those two attributes in his public image, forceful energy and innovative, if not radical, ideas.

In the summer of 1940 Reuther happened to drive past a new Packard aircraft engine plant being built as part of the government's rearmament program. France had fallen to the Nazis. England was prostrate and as good as beaten. The Soviet Union was a non-belligerent ally of Germany. The Nazi war machine had apparently won the war. Thousands of Americans suddenly felt alone and unusually insecure in a hostile world. Reuther knew, as he passed the preliminary concrete-pouring for the Packard plant, that no aircraft engines could be expected from it for eighteen months. When Reuther next talked to Sidney Hillman of the CIO, then with the newly created Office of Production Management of the U.S. Government, he described his thoughts as he had passed the new Packard plant. The leisurely pace of rearmament made no sense to Reuther. Hitler would not obligingly wait eighteen months or more. Reuther, more or less off the top of his head, suggested to Hillman that the idle productive capacity of Detroit's automobile plants might be able to produce military aircraft immediately. Hillman told Reuther to proceed, to make a study, and to develop his idea. From such accidental origins sprang Reuther's widely discussed and controversial "500 Planes a Day" plan.

By the time Reuther was ready to present a formal statement of his plan it had become something more considerable than a top-of-the-head idea. He first put UAW shop stewards and local officers to

60

work making statistical studies of factory floor space, idle machinery resources, and available skilled labor. He became convinced as he immersed himself in the reams of reports that his plan would work. He then had a persuasive and reasoned statement of the plan written and published, the work being done primarily by Edward Levinson, the CIO editor, and I. F. Stone, the liberal journalist. Philip Murray presented the plan to Franklin D. Roosevelt shortly before Christmas, 1940. Roosevelt evinced genuine interest, and he brought it to the attention of his advisers.

The Reuther plan touched off a lively, sometimes acrimonious debate. Even R. J. Thomas, the UAW president and Reuther's chief, had greeted the first suggestions of the plan with the disdain of a "pure and simple" union leader. "You're not going to make a horse's ass out of me. Stick to your knitting," he told Reuther. Among those in the labor movement who shared Thomas' pragmatic and job-limited interests, Reuther began to be viewed as a self-aggrandizing glamour boy, a grandstander. Managers in the automobile industry thought very much the same way about Reuther and his plan. When William Knudsen of General Motors, serving on the Office of Production Management with Sidney Hillman, was pressed to explain his objection to the plan, he replied testily, "I'm against it. It just won't work. Gentlemen, where I come from, when I say a thing won't work—*it don't work*." Charles E. Wilson, the chief executive of General Motors, responded to the plan with a counter proposal. "If Walter is interested in production, we'll give him a job with us."

The controversial nub of Reuther's plan, as far as management was concerned, resided in the role to be assigned to organized labor in the planning of production. The prospect of giving unions any say in management decisions was, of course, anathema. Whether or not the plan would actually work, whether or not it really was practical, was not the most interesting question about it in the collective mind of management. They categorically opposed the insinuating idea of worker representation and the erosion of their prerogatives. As one Roosevelt adviser remarked about the plan, the biggest thing wrong with it was where it had come from.

After Pearl Harbor the Reuther "500 Planes a Day" plan gradually died. For a brief period, before civilian production ceased almost entirely and before war production took over the industry, the Reuther plan hung in the balance. There was no *other* plan immediately available. Reuther, for the first time, became a familiar name and face among the very top echelons of power in America. Donald

Nelson, who succeeded Knudsen as industry's chief adviser to the government on the new War Production Board, summed up the impact Reuther had had. "He's quite a fellow. . . . Three-fourths of the dollar-a-year men around this place are scared to death of that little fellow. And, you know, they ought to be scared of him—because he's smarter than they are."

During the war years Reuther proposed another plan—or delivered himself of a brainstorm, as the case might be—which failed implementation as completely as his 1940-41 aircraft production plan. But again he enhanced his reputation as a creative and innovative labor leader. Reuther proposed what he called an "Equality of Sacrifice" plan. It involved ten proposals, the principal one being a ceiling on all private incomes at $25,000. Mrs. Roosevelt hailed the idea in her column "My Day." President Roosevelt included the ceiling idea in a wartime economic program he sent to Congress, although Congress paid little attention to it. Although the plan won wide currency among liberals and radicals to the further blossoming of Reuther's reputation, it served mostly as a political expedient for Reuther and the UAW leadership to get out of a dilemma they faced, namely, how to defend the "no strike" pledge to the rank and file, and to sweeten the other asceticisms of the war period, without seeming insensitive to rank and file discontents.

The war years accumulated a tremendous pressure of dammed-up frustrations among ordinary union men and women. Disarmed of their strike weapon by the patriotic "no strike" pledge, workers watched the inexorable wartime inflation diminish their nominally high wages. In the middle of the war the Government relented on its wage controls and permitted wage increases of up to fifteen percent, the so-called "Little Steel Formula." Labor economists, however, contested the figures of Government economists that the inflation had not been much in excess of the fifteen percent of the Little Steel Formula. Moreover, as war production began to taper off with the anticipated end of the war in late 1944 and 1945, the workers were denied extra income from overtime work.

In June, 1945, Reuther sent a report to the Office of War Mobilization and Reconversion, the War Labor Board, and the Office of Price Administration in which he argued the thesis that the automobile industry could pay a 30% increase in wages without the need also to raise its prices on automobiles. Reuther believed that his proposal met all the requirements of the general guidelines laid down in an earlier speech by President Truman. The President had hoped that no wage raises would be granted which would lead to increases in prices. By now, of course, Reuther was firmly established in the public imagination as an irrepressible gadfly, a genius and champion of the workers in the view from one gallery, a dangerous and demagogic radical in the view from another gallery.

As usual Reuther marshalled his facts and presented formidable documentary evidence to support his brilliant—or outrageous—demand. The UAW published and circulated widely Reuther's little booklet, *Purchasing Power for Prosperity: The Case of the General Motors Workers for Maintaining Take-Home Pay*. In the midst of the hot debate Reuther dropped his really disruptive bombshell, his "Look at the Books" challenge. He offered, at least implicitly, to lower his 30% wage increase demand if the corporation would open its books to permit an impartial audit to test his contention that a 30% increase could be granted without the necessity of raising prices. Again his proposal was greeted by some as brilliant, by others as outrageous. General Motors, of course, was particularly outraged at this attempt to penetrate the sacred realm of private enterprise.

In November, 1945, the UAW went out on strike against General Motors Corporation, following a "one at a time" strategy advocated by Reuther over some considerable opposition within the union. Reuther knew that the temporary immunity from the strike enjoyed by Ford, Chrysler, and the other companies, meant very little. If General Motors fell, the other companies would have to come around. About 200,000 automobile workers in General Motors plants left their jobs, and they stayed out for a long, difficult 113 days.

During the almost four months of the strike the nation argued and discussed the Reuther challenge. President Truman established a factfinding board of eminent citizens, which, although failing to end the strike, gave some implicit respectability to Reuther's "Open the Books" challenge by implying that the "facts," whatever they were, might have some bearing on the 30% wage increase demand. Management, of course, sturdily denied the connection, finding the principal meaning of the strike to reside in Reuther's "socialistic" demand. The conservative and liberal press discussed these implications at great length during the long winter of the strike. But, as one Socialist historian of the UAW has contended, only Reuther and his machine of ex-Socialists in the UAW, as well as the consistent conservatives on the executive councils of General Motors, really understood the implications of Reuther's challenge. The commercial press and the liberals failed to appreciate the radical implications of the strike, arguing superficially, for example, over the question whether a "look at the books" would support Reuther's claim or not. The rest of the labor movement showed a noticeable lack of interest in the dispute. To ordinary bread and butter unionists the issue seemed involved, "intellectual," and clearly secondary to simple wage issues. R. J. Thomas, for example, barely concealed his impatience with the whole issue as the strike continued week after week, and after an 18½ cent formula became available to the automobile workers, as to other workers, for the taking.

The "Communist"-led factional opponents of Reuther saw the long and complicated strike as an opportunity to undercut his power and prestige, especially in the face of growing incomprehension among rank and file strikers of what exactly was delaying a settlement. Other CIO unions began to accept, in their contract negotiations around actual or threatened strikes, an 18½ cent wage increase, reluctantly permitted by the Truman Administration, with no attached anti-inflationary prohibitions on price increases, and with no "intellectual" gibberish about "looking at the books." In particular, the Communist-led Electrical Workers Union accepted such a wage increase and began that serious isolation even within the ranks of labor of Reuther and the UAW. Reuther finally had to capitulate. Disappointed by his failure to achieve the central demand of the strike but nonetheless with a substantial wage increase to satisfy his constituency, he made much in the next several years of this undercutting of the strike by the Communists. He also remarked, in a more ironic vain, that it had taken General Motors *and* the Communist Party in unlikely coalition to defeat him.

The "500 Planes a Day" plan of 1940 and 1941 made Reuther, as we have seen, something more than an ordinary labor leader. He established himself, if only on a small beachhead, as a political force with influence in the Democratic Party. By the time of the General Motors strike in 1945 and his elevation to the presidency of the UAW in 1946 he had considerably widened that beachhead in American politics. By virtue of his factional anti-Communism within the UAW he quickly became a national leader of the liberal and Left anti-Communist forces in American politics of that budding Cold War era. He joined with others of like mind—prominent journalists and writers, other labor leaders in the Democratic Party, former Socialists and radicals—to isolate Communists and then to eliminate them from opinion-making organizations, labor unions, political parties and caucuses, veteran organizations, universities and colleges, and most "public" areas of American life. Reuther's factional fight within the UAW became almost a prototype for similar "educational" anti-Communist programs in other organizations in American society.

By 1950 anti-Communism had become something more than the understandable aversion of most Americans for the style and substance of Joseph Stalin's Soviet Union. It had taken on that gem-like glow of unquestioned orthodoxy, with liberal and conservative denominations, to be sure, but nonetheless a monolithic faith with a few basic tenets. Most Americans came to see the very meaning of their times as a great struggle for world hegemony between "Communism" and "freedom." The Soviet Union led the hard disciplined forces of the former; the United States led the less disciplined but more attractive Eagle Scout forces of the latter. The general staff of the enemy was something called "the international Communist conspiracy," and its capital was in Russia. There Joseph Stalin—at least until his death in 1953—directed his dedicated agents scattered all over the world, sending directives to Mao Tse-Tung, ordering Ho Chi Minh to action or inaction in Indochina, writing the campaign speeches for Italian Communist politicians, and even telling George Addes in the UAW how to proceed at conventions to "capture" the union. Described thus, the anti-Communist orthodoxy of American politics in the 1950's might seem over-simple and incredible. Obviously the basic catechismal items as here described were subject to complex variations to take into account such early and non-confirming realities as Stalin's cynicism in 1944 in dividing the world with Winston Churchill at the expense, if necessary, of Communist Parties; or Tito's successful defection in 1948. In general, it could be said that all Americans seemed to accept *some* variant of the model as being the axiomatic truth. On the Left, anti-Communists such as Reuther came to claim the most subtle and sophisticated version. They cited, with footnotes to real facts, their long history of actual contact with Communists. The liberals and radicals—whether or not they were ex-Communists themselves—claimed superior knowledge of the conspiracy. They even patronized somewhat the solid and old-fashioned anti-Communism of such American leaders as President Eisenhower or John Foster Dulles. The conservatives were right, of course, but their comparative ignorance of the enemy made them sometimes do tactically inappropriate and stupid things. For the anti-Communists on the extreme Right, such as Senator Joseph McCarthy or Robert Welch of the John Birch Society, the anti-Communist Left had only contempt. All that could possibly be said in extenuation for all that hysteria from the Right was, alas, that Communist successes in the 1930's and 1940's had somehow made

65

such a reaction inevitable among the hoi polloi. Indeed, the extreme Right only made it harder for the sophisticated and knowledgeable anti-Communist to do his job precisely and surgically. "McCarthyism" tended to give anti-Communism itself a bad name with responsible people, who found simply incredible the imprecise charges that the whole New Deal had been part of the "conspiracy," or that Eisenhower was a conscious agent of the "conspiracy."

In the 1970's, hardly a generation later, the whole post-World War II period of the domestic Cold War has taken on a new coloration. Younger historians, who study the period as historians rather than autobiographers, have not necessarily rehabilitated Joseph Stalin and his followers in the UAW as anything but the political toadies and sycophants most of them were, but they have suddenly illumined the whole mythological and "ideological" basis of the period, that tempting and over-simple Manichaeanism to which the hard facts of world history and personal experience gave credibility and drama.

Writing in a Preface to a 1957 study of Communism in the CIO by a colleague of his in the Americans for Democratic Action, liberal Senator Hubert H. Humphrey of Minnesota said, "The Communist infiltration of the CIO was a direct threat to the survival of all of our country's democratic institutions. The CIO victory over the Communist party was a significant victory for our nation. It was a crucial defeat for the international Communist conspiracy. . . . It [the story] should be told and retold, for it is a story of American men and women, members and leaders of our trade unions, and their successful struggle against our totalitarian enemies. . . ."

It is not now so much Senator Humphrey's facts that are in dispute—i.e., "totalitarian enemies," "Communist infiltration," "international Communist conspiracy"—but his tone, his hushed reading of the facts, his air of religious prejudgement, and his implicit call for commitment to some imprecise faith. Ironically, in hindsight, the liberal anti-Communist demanded of the labor movement a basic and "ideological" commitment to beliefs as extraneous to simple "pork chop" unionism as were the demands of the Communists. Even the most evangelical of the liberal anti-Communist historians of the CIO-Communist Party conflict admits that the "Communist-controlled" unions were indistinguishable from the purer unions in the manner in which they conducted their day-to-day union business and in the manner in which they conducted collective bargaining. Whatever the Communists wanted from American labor unions it apparently was not social revolution *by* the labor unions.[1]

66

Reuther probably became an anti-Communist by conviction years before it became the political orthodoxy of the whole country. The break-up of the Unity caucus in 1937 and 1938, and the Communists' withholding of support for him in the Michigan CIO election in 1938 may have predisposed Reuther to re-examine his youthful Socialist "ecumenism." He became quite visible as an anti-Communist in the 1941 convention of the UAW. He moved to deny appointive or elective office in the UAW to "Fascists or Communists," to anyone owing first allegiance to a "foreign government." The motion stirred a vigorous floor debate that lasted for more than two hours. The Communists made an amendment to the motion to include members of the Socialist Party in the ban. They also presented a minority report to the report of the Resolution Committee which had authored the Reuther motion. "The real question here," their minority report charged, "is whether the Socialist Party in the form of the Reuthers is going to have a privileged position in the union." The Reuther forces deflected that objection by pointing out, accurately enough, that the Socialist Party, whatever it might be, was hardly the "agent for a foreign government," and consequently in an entirely different category from the banned organizations. The Communists then attacked Reuther as a draft evader, descending as was sometimes their wont to the personal level. Reuther explained his deferment, as he thereafter had to do frequently. He had not himself requested the deferment, he said. Philip Murray and R. J. Thomas had requested it for him from his local draft board, and the deferment had been granted because of his essential work for war production.

After his second successful campaign for the presidency of the UAW in 1947 and his subsequent purge of Communists from the UAW, Reuther joined with other anti-Communist leaders of CIO unions to press for a purification of the CIO. At the 1949 CIO convention Reuther and Murray sponsored together an expulsion of eleven unions from the federation, including the United Electrical Workers and the United Farm Equipment Union, unions with which Reuther, as we have seen, had come into conflict in his own career. At the 1950 convention of the CIO in Chicago not a single Communist or Communist-liner attended. William Z. Foster, chief of the American Communist Party, gave his loser's interpretation of the purge by charging that the "process of transforming the CIO top bureaucratic machine into a tool of the State Department was complete."

The Americans for Democratic Action, which Reuther helped to found in early 1947, became the general staff for the new anti-

Communist Left in America. It organized itself to purify the whole New Deal reform tradition of the taint of Communist "totalitarianism," to block the Communist-supported—and perhaps Communist-instigated—Presidential campaign of Henry A. Wallace on the Progressive Party ticket in 1948, to organize critical support from the Left for Truman-era Cold War policies such as the Truman Doctrine or the Marshall Plan or the North Atlantic Treaty Organization. Reuther exercised considerable power and leverage through this movement and through his access to Democratic Party leaders. Although the final judgment—if there can ever be such a thing—of Reuther as an anti-Communist national leader must wait longer, it is already clear, at the very least, that he consistently proposed the most humanistic and progressive means of coping with the amorphous ideological enemy. He never jettisoned the social democracy of his father and grandfather, the belief that evil would not be defeated by guns or counter-tyranny but only by continuing the good fight for the material well-being of the disadvantaged, and for the growth of freedom which the very fight entailed.

In April, 1948, Reuther received two threatening letters. One anonymous correspondent took exception to his anti-Communism. The other objected just as vehemently to his public endorsement some days earlier of racial integration in bowling tournaments. As a famous and highly controversial person, Reuther took no particular note of the letters, although they certainly presented him with evidence that some persons hated him with a fury.

On April 20, 1948, Reuther telephoned to his wife, May, during a late afternoon executive board meeting in a downtown Detroit hotel that he would be late for supper. After the long meeting, he and an assistant drove to the UAW headquarters to complete some minor business. At 8:30 Reuther drove home to his modest six room bungalow on the northwest side of Detroit. When he arrived home he ate his warmed-over stew while standing at the kitchen breakfast bar. He then went to the refrigerator for some cooled peaches, and as he opened the door he turned half around to answer some casual question put to him by May Reuther. At that instant he was struck by five pellets from the blast of a 12 gauge shotgun fired at him through the kitchen window. Four of the pellets tore into his right arm, causing severe damage to the radial nerve. The fifth pellet lodged in his chest. His turning to answer May's question had prevented him from receiving the full blast of the shotgun in the chest.

Surgeons labored over Reuther for more than two hours as they

68

tried to repair the arm, which had dangled as if held by only a few threads during the race to the hospital. The Reuther house by morning was a tourist attraction, with even a popcorn vendor on hand to serve the crowd. The house and the family, and Reuther in the hospital, were put under heavy guard. Eventually, the house had to be sold, and the family moved to another closer to UAW headquarters, a house with a high protective fence and bright protective lights around it.

Reuther fought hard for the use of his arm, as he had fought for the restoration of his big toe back in the Wheeling Steel Company plant. His recovery was complicated. He contracted both hepatitis and malaria from the frequent blood transfusions. He countermanded the doctors who told him he had only the choice of what position he wanted his permanently immobilized arm to be set in. In November, months after the attack, he suffered five hours of new surgery as neurological surgeons tried to piece together the minute shreds of the damaged radial nerve. He was given odds of a million to one on the use of his arms. But he worked assiduously at his therapy. Eighteen months after the attack he experienced the triumph of discovering that he could just barely move his thumb.

In May, 1949, Victor Reuther was shot in the living room of his house. Again the assassin had crept to the window and fired through the glass. Surgeons were forced to remove Victor's right eye.

Twenty years later, in April, 1968, the statute of limitations on the crime ran out, and without any solution. Reuther was obviously not disinterested in the inconclusive sleuthing that followed the assassination attempt. But he characteristically did not permit himself to get side-tracked into any preoccupation with personal revenge. He speculated that the attempt on his life could have come from Communists, the underworld, or certain "die hard" elements among the employers. And he left it more or less at that. He said: "I, in effect, as a part of one's own peace of mind, sort of intellectually decided that why should I try to be a Sherlock Holmes and try to solve this crime, and get myself so deeply emotionally involved that I'm doing *that* rather than doing the things I want to do."

With his principal enemies subdued—the intransigent "open shop" corporations of the automobile industry and the Communists and "Communists" within the UAW and the CIO—Reuther became in 1948 and into the 1960's the far-sighted and creative institutionalizer of the labor revolution of the 1930's, the revolution he had also helped to make. Even from our limited perspective of the 1970's he seems to have achieved an important and secure place for himself as a labor statesman. Without immersing ourselves in the minutiae of his career as a negotiator, we can at least trace some of his innovations in labor relations for which he will probably be remembered. In a few of the early negotiations it must be granted that Reuther had the historical good fortune to be contending with an extraordinary opponent, Charles E. Wilson, the chief executive of General Motors. In popular history Wilson is remembered as the politically unsophisticated Secretary of Defense in Eisenhower's cabinet who created little political crises for the President by crassly identifying the interests of General Motors with the interests of the United States of America, or by comparing unemployed workers who demanded help from the government to dependent and un-enterprising kennel dogs. But in his proper milieu, which was not political administration, he proved to be intelligent, and as adaptive and innovative as his principal opponent, Walter Reuther. Indeed, the two men developed an unlikely personal attachment and often-times met socially, or conversed for half an hour or longer on the telephone.

Wilson, in fact, should probably get the historical credit for the novel features of the 1948 contract between the UAW and General Motors. The "escalator clause" provided for an increase in workers' wages based on increased productivity, and the "cost of living formula" provided for an increase of one cent an hour for each advance of 1.14 points on the cost of living index of the Bureau of Labor Statistics. In 1948 the two ideas were new and revolutionary. Reuther, of course, was recuperating from the assassination attempt and obviously could play only a passive and indirect role in the negotiations. Wilson presented the plan, which the UAW negotiators accepted quickly. But perhaps a kind of historic distribution of gold stars can be made. Although Wilson advanced the idea in the 1948 talks, he admitted he had been converted to the basic idea by the arguments of Reuther in the earlier 1945-46 strike. Twenty years later Reuther estimated that the "escalator clause" alone had given $18,000 dollars to the average full-time automobile worker, and all quite automatically, without struggles or strikes.

Reuther could take more unshared credit for another innovation in collective bargaining with which his name is linked: automobile workers' pensions. He introduced the idea first in 1947 in negotiations with Ford. The time was not quite ripe for serious negotiation or agreement, but the seed of the idea had become firmly implanted. Reuther argued and propagandized for the idea assiduously during the next several years. "If you make $258 an hour, they give it to you. If you make $1.65 an hour, they say to you, 'you don't need it; you can't have it; we're not going to give it to you.' " He also coined the phrase, later worked into a labor "folksong," "too old to work; too young to die."

In 1949 Ford agreed to the first funded pension plan in the industry, which guaranteed workers with thirty years service a minimum pension, including normal Social Security benefits, of $100 a month. Unlike the earlier pension plan of the United Mine Workers, Reuther insisted that the Ford plan be "funded," financed out of a set-aside fund. The United Mine Workers pension, of course, was to be paid out of current royalties on tons of coal mined, and in a few years time was to run into financial difficulties.

To achieve the same kind of pension plan for Chrysler workers the UAW called a strike which dragged on for 104 days. It proved a severe test of workers' devotion to Reuther's somewhat abstract, "intellectual" ideas. Strikers even began to make a joke out of Reuther's phrase, "actuarially sound," which they barely understood.

In 1950 Reuther agreed in contract negotiations with General Motors to an unprecedented five-year contract. Again Reuther was hailed as a labor leader of unusual perspicacity and imagination. The contract, of course, suited the purposes of both parties. The renewed cost of living agreement of 1948 and the "escalator clause" protected the UAW, seemingly, against pressures of inflation. But the Korean War and its unusual inflationary pressures interrupted the anticipated five years of peace. In 1952, and into 1953, Reuther agitated for a re-negotiation of the contract. Extraordinary and unforeseen conditions had intervened, he argued. A labor contract should be viewed as "a living document," not a ball and chain on either party. Reuther made his argument persuasive with a series of wildcat strikes, slow-downs, and such carefully programmed persuaders. Although General Motors shouted indignantly, "Breach of contract!", the company nevertheless agreed in 1953 to new talks and to a wage increase above the contract obligations of 1950.

By the early 1950's Reuther began to propagandize, in speeches, magazine and press articles, and interviews, for an idea which came to be labeled the "guaranteed annual wage." The idea, however, did not appear in serious contract negotiations till early 1955. The contracts with both Ford and General Motors were scheduled to expire in May, 1955, the General Motors contract about a week before the Ford contract. Reuther permitted a week's extension of the General Motors contract because he had chosen to make the negotiations with Ford the arena for the conflict over his guaranteed annual wage, and because he saw the advantage of driving a tactical wedge between the corporations. Ford, as he had expected, offered a limited guaranteed annual wage plan to avoid a strike. It hardly met the UAW specifications, but it was the first concession on the question made by any company, and Reuther accepted it. Ford agreed to set aside 5c an hour for every worker to provide a fund to pay up to 25c an hour for twenty-six weeks for every worker laid off. The plan, of course, assumed and built into government unemployment insurance. Together the two payments to a laid off worker would pay him up to 65% of his regular wages for up to half a year.

Although this initial guaranteed wage contract with Ford was really more of a guaranteed half year's partial wages, the UAW was happy with the breakthrough. The modest guarantee had its big test in the recession of 1958 and supplied some economic cushion to thousands of workers laid off for unusually long periods in that bad year. The UAW also kept improving the program in subsequent contract negotiations with Ford and the other companies. By 1967 the guarantee offered the more or less permanently employed automobile worker up to 95% of his regular pay for up to a full year if he were laid off. It even began to be referred to as "rocking chair money," and conservative I-told-you-so critics of the whole idea charged that automobile workers began to compete with each other for the privilege of being laid off.

In 1961 the UAW signed an intricate profit-sharing contract with American Motors which seemed to take cognizance of the fact that the workers in smaller automobile companies in the oligopolistic industry had a vested interest in the continued existence and economic health of their employers. American Motors and the UAW agreed that the first 10% of net profits should go to stockholders. The next 15% was to be set aside in a workers' fund, earmarked for various purposes such as workers' pensions and unemployment benefits.

It is apparent that Reuther came to his job as labor negotiator with new and interesting ideas. He was no simple power broker, or "pork chopper," who considered his job well done if he succeeded in pressuring employers into granting "his men" periodic wage increases. But by the 1960's even Reuther seemed to have run out of really new ideas. Of course he worked assiduously for refinements and perfections in the ideas he had first breached in the 1940's or 1950's, such as the guaranteed annual wage, pensions, or automatic productivity increases in pay. In fact, we might see an attenuation of his earlier Socialist hopes and strategies. His 1940 plan to insinuate labor unions into management decisions and his disingenuous requests in 1945 that management "open its books" were, in retrospect, his most "Socialistic" demands. With such demands he seemed to have been demanding for labor something approaching "co-determination," a program advanced with great fanfare by West German unions and the Social Democratic Party after World War II. Novel and interesting as his subsequent demands of the 1950's were, they hardly implied such institutional changes in the whole structure of American business.

In 1952 the election of Dwight D. Eisenhower to the Presidency shocked both the AFL and the CIO. Neither of the labor federations had supported the candidacy of Eisenhower. Then, within two weeks of the election, both federations lost their own presidents. Philip Murray died at the age of sixty-six. William Green of the AFL died twelve days later at the age of eighty-two. The CIO postponed its already scheduled convention for a two weeks' period of mourning. Amid the sincere mourning, however, the politics of succession began. Reuther was obviously the strongest candidate to succeed Murray, although he was opposed by another candidate from Murray's CIO executive board whose real support derived from Murray's successor as president of the Steel Workers, David J. McDonald. But Reuther could not be blocked, and in December, 1952, at the Atlantic City CIO convention he became the third president of the CIO. The convention unveiled considerable personal animosity but scarcely any of the ideological controversy of the "old days." The impression left in the minds of even Reuther's warmest supporters by the convention was that he was admired and trusted but scarcely liked. When McDonald of the Steel Workers tried to bury the hatchet by saying, "Well, at least we got to like each other better," Reuther responded honestly but with little warmth, "No, David, we got to *know* each other better." The convention ended on a somewhat heavy-handed and forced light note, with Reuther being ordered by the convention to smoke a cigar and drink a beer for every one of his votes. Reuther begged off, pleading physical incapacity.

In the meantime George Meany succeeded to the presidency of the AFL. Desultory talks and wishful thinking about the desirability of a reunification of the AFL and CIO had been present since the break. Now such a reunification seemed feasible and more than ever desirable. Two days after his election Meany arranged a personal conference with Reuther. The talks, proposals, and counter-proposals began in earnest. The practical problems of jurisdictions, personal precedence, career conflicts, and constitutional protection for existing unions were formidable.

Arthur Goldberg, the CIO counsel and subsequent Supreme Court Justice and UN Ambassador, drew up a detailed plan of merger early in 1955 for presentation to an AFL executive council meeting scheduled to meet in Miami Beach in February. Reuther attended the conference, after first making public his general disapproval of labor leaders meeting in such sybaritic splendor in Miami Beach, like corporation plutocrats on expense accounts. At the meeting Reuther addressed the AFL chieftains with what became his usual speech on the philosophy and mission of the labor movement. He was received politely. Meany then summed up the practical problems of merger in four short sentences and accepted Arthur Goldberg's draft proposal.

In the new AFL-CIO, the CIO was to be the noticeable junior partner. The AFL dominated the new joint executive board. Reuther, in fact, became technically only one among twenty-six other vice-presidents, although his prestige and reputation obviously made him first among equals. Also, he became head of the new Industrial Union Department within the merged federation, composed almost entirely of all the old CIO unions with a few newcomers like the Teamsters Union carefully screened by Reuther who acted in this bailiwick like a one-man credentials committee. In December, 1955, Reuther and Meany ceremoniously gavelled the first unity convention into session, both grasping the huge gavel and smiling into the cameras.

Reuther may have accepted his something less than equal footing in the new merged AFL-CIO because he anticipated the presidency for himself when the older George Meany retired or died. Also, his heart still belonged primarily to the UAW, as it had even during the brief period of his tenure as CIO president. At any rate, Reuther never seemed completely at home in his new command post, as a dignitary of the new AFL-CIO. As the gadfly and "radical" on the executive board he was the constant subject of press rumors about his disaffection, and about his conflicts over philosophy and politics with Meany.

By 1955 Reuther had reached the apex of his career. The last fifteen years of his life, busy and influential as they undoubtedly were, seem an anti-climax. He continued, of course, to be a force in the Democratic Party, and his support and endorsement were eagerly sought, from both John F. Kennedy and Hubert Humphrey in 1960 to all the hopefuls in the 1968 nomination race. At several points in his career, mostly early, he had toyed with the idea of lending his support to a new "labor" third party to try to bring about a basic re-alignment of the stalemated American party system, a tempting idea that even Franklin D. Roosevelt had played with after the 1940 election. But Reuther only considered the idea. Neither did he really encourage the few attempts made in his behalf to enter his name into the electoral arena of politics.

In 1966 he made a sentimental journey to the Soviet Union to revisit the Gorki automobile plant where he and his brother had worked over thirty years before. Apparently no outraged and deserted wife named "N" was waiting for him. Also the bitter debate at the dinner table with Khrushchev seemed forgotten by both himself and his hosts. He reported that he was particularly pleased to find that, even after twenty years of Cold War, the Russians still kept the little American flags and the plaques expressing gratitude for the equipment received in Lend-Lease aid during the Second World War. Reuther was anything but an introspective man, but the trip must have nudged even him into complicated reflections on the long road he had travelled since he had last seen Gorki, on the brevity of human life, on the vicissitudes of history. His early and juvenile enthusiasm for the "socialism" of the Soviet Union had undergone vast and complicated changes, as the Soviet Union itself had. But did he still see the labor movement, in 1966, as the instrument of human progress and freedom? If he reflected on the impermanence of things and came to doubt, did he admit his doubts to himself?

By the 1950's intellectuals were saying that the labor movement had won all its historical battles, that the old war was now over. The United States had come through into "affluence," and labor had been both author and beneficiary of the breakthrough. But where did that success—and actual production workers in American industries might have taken the intellectuals to task for their too easy assumptions of utopia—leave such a labor revolutionist as Walter Reuther? If the new society had attained that magic "fifth stage" of economic development and if all that remained were "technical" problems of "public sector" versus "private sector" investment, what role remained for the labor movement? Labor leaders perforce must become merely power brokers, meeting in Miami Beach on lavish expense accounts to try to raise the wages for their already "affluent" mechanics and wage earners so that they could buy their second television sets and their motor boats for their guaranteed vacations with pay. Although that picture of the 1950's, of an "end to ideology," now seems unreal, it had some slight basis in reality. The new poor and disadvantaged were not so much exploited workers as of old, requiring organization to exert pressure for the amelioration of their lot, but the redundant or superfluous poor trapped without function in decaying big cities for whom the traditional methods of labor organizing had little applicability.

Reuther apparently coped with this problem, this insidious feeling that his skills, experience, and the philosophy of labor union action might not be appropriate to the new age. He devoted more and more of his time to liberal causes. He marched in the Selma, Alabama, demonstration that marked the high point of the early Civil Rights revolution. He threw his considerable influence in the Democratic Party behind more and better ameliorative governmental "programs," whether in public health, housing, urban renewal, conservation, or racial justice. He advised liberally as always on the correct macro-economic policies to pursue for insurance of prosperity and full employment. He seemed to welcome Cesar Chavez's militant union of agricultural workers because it showed the country, and Reuther himself, that unionism was still relevant, still responsive to the needs of the poor and exploited. He was the only major AFL-CIO leader who gave his unstinting "visible" support to that heroic unionization drive of the 1960's.

Still, when young radicals at an environmental teach-in in Ann Arbor in the spring of 1970 listened to Reuther's usual impassioned speech, they caught and reflected none of his passion. They egged him on, as a lark. And Reuther apparently did not know he was being teased.

"It was sad as hell to watch," said one reporter.[2]

The hecklers, cruel and ignorant as they undoubtedly were, nevertheless demonstrated that hungry generations tread us all down, that even history-makers are superseded by history. But the hecklers, of course, were subject to the same obsolescence they found amusing in Reuther. Considering the stature of the man they teased, the joke, if any, in that sad confrontation was on them.

NOTES

CHAPTER ONE

[1] The most reliable source on Reuther's early years is: Frank Cormier and William J. Eaton, *Reuther* (Englewood Cliffs, N. J.: Prentice-Hall, Inc., 1970), Chaps. I and II. Many of the stories of his youth also have been told and retold in the various "profiles" and thumbnail sketches appearing in magazines during his lifetime.

[2] This part of the record of the UAW convention has been reprinted in: Paul F. Douglass, "Walter P. Reuther: Workers' Pressure toward Economic Security with Political Freedom," in *Six Upon the World: Toward an American Culture for an Industrial Age* (Boston: Little, Brown and Company, 1954), pp. 211-213.

CHAPTER TWO

[1] The longest, most "damaging" version of the "Vic and Wal" letter is reprinted in: Eldorous L. Dayton, *Walter Reuther: The Autocrat of the Bargaining Table* (New York: The Devin-Adair Co., 1958).

[2] For an interesting, and almost a contemporary account of the rise of the CIO, by a CIO editor, see: Edward Levinson, *Labor on the March* (New York: University Books, 1938; 1956).

CHAPTER THREE

[1] Irving Howe and E. J. Widick, *The UAW and Walter Reuther* (New York: Random House, 1949), pp. 3-44.

[2] This part of the Hearings of the NLRB is reprinted in: Cormier and Eaton, *op. cit.*, pp. 108-110.

CHAPTER FOUR

[1] Len De Caux, *Labor Radical: From the Wobblies to CIO* (Boston: Beacon Press, 1970), p. 256.

[2] A thoughtful history of these factional disputes and of Reuther's drive to the presidency of the UAW can be found in: Howe and Widick, *op. cit.*, pp. 149-171.

CHAPTER FIVE

[1] For almost a perfect example of liberal anti-Communism, including also the preface by Senator Hubert Humphrey, see: Max M. Kampelman, *The Communist Party vs. the CIO: A Study in Power Politics* (New York: Fred-

erick A. Praeger, 1957). For a different view of the same story see: Len De Caux, *op. cit.,* pp. 470-485.

[2] W. Serrin, "The Unknown Who Leads the Walter P. Reuther Memorial Strike," *New York Times Magazine*, September 27, 1970, p. 29.

BIBLIOGRAPHICAL ESSAY

For the most serious student of the career of Walter Reuther the first place to go is the Labor History Archives of the Wayne State University in Detroit. The Archives are the official repository of UAW and Reuther papers and materials, although most of the collection is not yet available to the public. But other related materials—papers and documents of the labor movement and UAW officials—are available. More accessible to the ordinary school researcher is the voluminous reportage in newspapers and magazines that accompanied Reuther's career from 1937 to 1970. The *New York Times* and the Detroit newspapers are obvious sources. The weekly news magazines and journals of opinion—from *Business Week* and *U.S. News and World Report* on the Right to *The Nation, New Republic, Commonweal, et al.,* on the liberal Left—are additional sources.

For a man of his importance Reuther generated few book-length biographies. The best is the most recent: Frank Cormier and William J. Eaton, *Reuther* (Englewood Cliffs, N. J.: Prentice-Hall, Inc., 1970). This biography is based on detailed, thorough research, and—for the time, at least—must be considered the definitive biography. Generally sympathetic, from a moderate Socialist point of view, is the older work: Irving Howe and E. J. Widick, *The UAW and Walter Reuther* (New York: Random House, 1949). A thoroughly unfriendly study, and oftentimes confused in its interpretations of the sectarianism of the Left, is: Eldorous L. Dayton, *Walter Reuther: The Autocrat of the Bargaining Table* (New York: The Devin-Adair Co., 1958). The other books are of more limited usefulness: Fred J. Cook, *Walter Reuther* (Chicago: Encyclopedia Britannica Press, 1963), and Paul F. Douglass, "Walter P. Reuther: Workers' Pressure toward Economic Security with Political Freedom," in *Six Upon the World: Toward an American Culture for an Industrial Age* (Boston: Little, Brown and Company, 1954).

The following list of books is the merest sample from a vast library on the American labor movement in general, the origins of the CIO, the problem of Communism in labor unions, and such matters touched upon in this brief biographical essay. Keith Sward,

The Legend of Henry Ford (New York: Rinehart and Co., 1948); Saul Alinsky, *John L. Lewis: An Unauthorized Biography* (New York: G. P. Putnam's Sons, 1949); Clayton W. Fountain, *Union Guy* (New York: The Viking Press, 1949); Foster Rhea Dulles, *Labor in America: A History*, Third Edition (New York: Thomas Y. Crowell Company, 1966); Edward Levinson, *Labor on the March* (New York: University Books, 1938; 1956); Max M. Kampelman, *The Communist Party vs. the CIO: A Study in Power Politics* (New York: Frederick A. Praeger, 1957); Len De Caux, *Labor Radical: From the Wobblies to CIO* (Boston: Beacon Press, 1970).